AWAY WITH THE VICAR

Margaret Walker

AWAY WITH THE VICAR

MARGARET WALKER

To my dear husband, Michael

UPFRONT PUBLISHING
PETERBOROUGH, ENGLAND

Away with the Vicar
Copyright © Margaret Walker 2007

All rights reserved.

ISBN 978-184426-452-0

First Published 2007 by
UPFRONT PUBLISHING LTD
Peterborough, England.

Printed by Printondemand-Worldwide Ltd.

To all who, along with me,
have gone away with the vicar.

Haven't we had fun?

Acknowledgements

To Michael for his love and a lifetime of
adventures without which there would have
been no material for another book.

To my nephew, Simon for suggesting
that I should write this book.

To our children, Christopher, Pauline
and Rosemary for their support.

To my publishing editor, another Simon for his
enthusiastic cooperation and to Gwynn Jones of
Porthmadog for the front cover photograph

Away with the Vicar

Margaret Walker

Chapter One

'Get out and climb into the back of the van!' he ordered. 'Sit on the right-hand side and hold on tight.'

Just 48 hours earlier I had promised to obey, so I slid to the ground, on my stiletto heels, opened the back doors and levered my seven and a half stone frame onto the mucky hump over the back wheel. I was wearing my red bouclé going away suit, with a squirrel collar. The suitcase with my honeymoon clothes had inadvertently been left at my parents' house. Hence my honeymoon wardrobe consisted of spare pants and a pair of gardening boots. Soon, I had thought, we would be in Scotland where I would buy a cheap skirt and walking shoes. But travelling from our new home in York over the Pennines towards Carlisle there was a loud bang. The back spring of our van had broken.

Michael had bought 'the van' – a blue Morris 8 – from Bootle Press for £18 when he was at theological college in Birkenhead. With the help of fellow students he had replaced its engine with one bought from a scrapyard. The work took place at the side of the college chapel, to the consternation of the principal. At the end of term the principal ended his personal interview with Michael with the prayer: 'Dear God, please help Michael to realise that he came to study theology at St. Aidan's, and not car maintenance. Amen.'

The van had passed its MOT, but when stopped for a spot check at the exit to the Mersey tunnel it had refused to start as the battery was flat. The police were understanding and stopped all the traffic in the tunnel so that they could push the blue van backwards to get it started. Michael then drove non-stop to Newcastle-upon-Tyne to visit me – his fiancée. The van had thereafter proved quite reliable – that was until our honeymoon.

We staggered down in our broken-springed van to the nearest town, Kirkby Stephen, where we realised we couldn't afford to stay in the 3-star hotel. However we found a Cyclists' Touring Club hotel which purported to be closed for the season but where the proprietor took pity on us and offered us two metal hospital beds in the attic. I noted wryly that it was called 'The Temperance Hotel'. That was one virtue we didn't expect to have to exercise on our honeymoon!

The next morning we peered through October fog until we found a car scrapyard. Michael poked around flea-ridden wrecks to find a spring that could be salvaged. My stilettos sank into the mud and my squirrel collar hung limp with mist. By lunchtime the fog was clearing as I tottered into town, returning with fish and chips which I hand-fed to a greasy Michael on the scrapyard forecourt as he wielded spanners and wrenches to replace the broken spring. The lady at the

'Temperance' offered us another night's bed and breakfast and an evening meal for 15 shillings all in. We said goodbye to ideas of driving to Scotland and asked if we could stay in Kirkby Stephen for the rest of the week.

Each morning I would come downstairs wearing gardening boots and Michael's anorak, which were the nearest I could get to 'Walking round the Lake District' gear. In the evening I would change into my squirrel-collared jacket and stilettos. At night we pushed the hospital beds together in the attic. It wasn't what I had envisaged as a honeymoon boudoir. No fluffy carpets, soft lights or vases of roses. The itinerary was also widely divergent from what I had imagined. Two days were spent on Shap where Michael had eyes only for the steam engines; another day we walked on disused railway tracks and one day we investigated the engine sheds at Carlisle. I often think it was the fact that I had once had an Ian Allan train spotters' book (thanks to having six boy cousins) which had endeared me to Michael. The ability to identify an A3 engine and understand the meaning of a 4-6-0 wheel arrangement had registered me higher on the 'curate's wife' scale than had my ability to play the organ or recite 1 Corinthians 13 by heart. It had been no surprise to have my engagement ring thrust on the wrong finger of the wrong hand on Platform 8 South at York railway station, and then to have been abandoned while he ran off to platform 9 to view an A4 Pacific engine.

When our honeymoon week ended I signed the Temperance Hotel visitors' book 'The Revd. Michael and Mrs Margaret Walker'. That felt good. The proprietor's wife glanced over my shoulder and said, 'You must have such a demanding life – no wonder you look so tired.' She obviously had no idea that we had been on our honeymoon – and I could quite see why. After all, most new brides have rather more clothes in their suitcase, and they don't go out hiking wearing squirrel collars and gardening boots.

We nurtured our newly-sprung van gently over the Pennines back into Yorkshire, ready to settle down to our first curacy days in a parish on the outskirts of York. After a honeymoon with a difference I began to wonder if being a curate's wife was going to be different from my teenage imaginings. I had met Michael in 1958 when his father had come to be the vicar of St. Mary's church in Beverley where I was a bell-ringer. Yes, we had first met in the belfry, which may explain a thing or too! Three weeks after meeting each other we left Beverley. Michael went to Lampeter to study History, English, and Classics, while I went to Nottingham to study Social Administration. Over the next two years we wrote to one another in term-time and met up in the vacations. Friendship burgeoned into romance. In our third year he hitchhiked to visit me in my 'digs' one very wet weekend in February. There, on my landlady's threadbare brown settee I found myself engaged to an ordinand. Michael now tells me that he actually said, 'You would make me a good vicar's wife.' I was certain that he had said a more generalized 'You would make a good vicar's wife.' To which I had replied, rather conceitedly, 'Yes.' He took this to be my acceptance of a marriage proposal and proceeded to smother me with kisses. I was wise not to tell him I had misunderstood his statement

I had another two years in which to fantasize about being the lady of the vicarage. The drawing room would have long velvet curtains and be lit by pink table lamps. Middle-aged and elderly ladies would come to discuss the Easter flower arrangements, after which I would wheel in cucumber sandwiches and fairy cakes on an elegant trolley. My husband might pop in, looking sleek and handsome in his black cassock, and my ivy-leafed teacup of joy would be full and running over. Surely goodness and loving kindness would follow us all the days of our vicarage life and we would dwell in this house of peace and well-being for ever.

Being disgorged from an ancient blue van outside a newly built semi, our first curate's house in York, was a far cry from such dreams. My suitcase of 'ordinary clothes' had been delivered, the red bouclé suit was put away, and I put on a sweater and skirt and apron to clean and organise our new home. Michael had been ordained in York Minster the month before and was soon immersed in staff meetings, visiting, sermon preparation and taking services. I had intended to have a month of 'home-making' before starting a job in a child psychiatry unit in York. We had been to auction sales and bought a double bed, a wardrobe and chest of drawers for £12, and had spent most of our savings on three small carpets. We would have bought four had not Michael made an extravagant purchase the week before the wedding.

With only £46 in the bank, which represented my savings from one year as a medical social worker in Sheffield, he had thought it appropriate to spend almost a quarter of it on a black, filthy, oily piece of scrap metal, offered to him by someone working for the railways in York. I was not amused. However, he insisted that it was a bargain, and that when it was degreased and polished I would love it. It was a solid brass engine nameplate from the A3 'St. Gatien', the same class as the 'Flying Scotsman'. How could I have ever doubted that this was a bargain? I helped to clean it so that it could stand on the ledge in our bay window looking out onto a new housing estate on the edge of York, and beyond to the London – Edinburgh line on which it had spent its 38 years of working life. We did some research and found it was named after a racehorse that had been joint winner of the Derby in 1884.

Two weeks after returning from honeymoon I burst into tears. I wasn't enjoying being a curate's wife. Michael didn't have much time at home. I didn't drive and was stuck in a cul-de-sac on the outskirts of York. I felt guilty that I had all that I had wanted – a handsome young curate husband, a new house and dozens of wonderful wedding presents to sort out, and yet I felt depressed. To make matters worse I was distinctly under the weather and had no enthusiasm for embarking into child psychiatry, or for visiting my new neighbours. Michael was sympathetic and put it down to the inevitable slump after the great build up of leaving my job in Sheffield, his ordination, our wedding and the house move.

Six weeks after the honeymoon I was admitted to hospital with stomach pains. The initial diagnosis was appendicitis. Fortunately the surgeon did not operate. After three days I was discharged and my GP came to see me. I obliged with a urine sample and he returned the next day with a huge grin on his face. I was pregnant. No wonder the lady at the Temperance Hotel had thought I had looked tired!

Kirkby Stephen. What a delightful place for a conception. If the baby were a boy he would have Stephen for one of his names. His grandpa would, of course, believe that he was called after him.

The parishioners were thrilled with the news and suddenly seemed more friendly. As they knitted and crocheted 58 matinée coats and cardigans, I managed to do some research into 'St Gatien' in between my many bouts of sickness. Yes, the nameplate had been made in honour of a racehorse, but the horse had been named after a saint – a patron saint of fertility!

Chapter Two

'Get me some lemonade! Now! Please!' It was 2 a.m. and it was my turn to give orders. There's no telling what cravings pregnancy brings. As I swigged down the fizzy nectar straight from the bottle with greedy gulps, I placated my long-suffering husband with the medical information that some women even ate coal.

'Just think what that would do to the sheets,' I said. But I did not stay smug for long. 'Get me the bowl, quick!'

The lemonade was making a quick return and endangering the pillow and the sheets. When the crisis was over I snuggled under the blankets and comforted myself with the thought that I wasn't an elephant. They have two years of being pregnant. On the other hand they probably don't suffer from morning sickness.

Why did they call it morning sickness, anyway? Mine was the 24-hour variety. My doctor said there was some new medication available to stave off my incessant bouts, but in the first instance he would prefer me to eat ginger biscuits and chew antacid tablets. I did as I was bidden, to little avail, but fortunately I did not press him for the magic new medication. Many years later I learned its name. Thalidomide.

'What size shoe do you take?' asked the doctor. He looked somewhat amazed when I said I took a 6 or 6½.

'Well, as you live fairly close to a hospital you can go for a home delivery, unless there are any complications.'

I had never realised there was a correlation between shoe size and pelvic girth. Now for the first time in my life I loved my big feet.

My bump grew bumpier and in accordance with the custom of the 1960s had to be hidden from public view. Nowadays the pendulum has swung to the uttermost extreme and I gaze at bare protruding stomachs, and navels complete with rings and studs, and think how close the noisy outside world must seem to their curled up embryos. Mine was shielded for nine months by voluminous pinafores and bell tent dresses, which were promptly torn up for use as polishing cloths once their prime duty was done.

The Mothers' Union clucked round me and showered me with advice. I had been enrolled as a member at the tender age of 24 and my vicar's wife had immediately asked me to form and lead a members' choir. After weeks of rehearsals we were assembled in the vestry, ready to process out for the opening hymn. As their leader I was at the front and as my bump came into the congregation's full view I realised that we were singing the words 'Come forth ye virgins wise'. I tried to concentrate on the alto line, and averted my eyes from Michael's giggles.

As well as being a curate, Michael was also part-time chaplain at what was then called Clifton Mental Hospital in York. In an effort to get to know both patients and staff better he decided to attend some of their social events. Bingo and whist did not appeal, so he opted for the fancy dress. The only trouble was that we hadn't yet amassed any dressing up clothes. Later on in his ministry we had trunks full of them and could turn out cowboys, angels, devils, rabbits, innkeepers and shepherds at a minute's notice. Who would help us out in York? The Sunday school superintendent seemed a good starting point. Michael had been sent to see her on the first day after his ordination. The vicar had heard that she was about to resign as she had received complaints from a mother about a boy who had put newts down her daughter's neck while waiting for Sunday school to begin. Terrified at the prospect of having to placate 'an old crone' and encourage her not to give up her godly calling, Michael nervously tapped the door.

'Come on in,' said a jolly young woman, brandishing a chip pan.

'I'm just doing egg and chips – would you like some?'

There began a friendship with Joan which still continues. By the time the last chip was eaten the angst over the newts had been swept aside and she remained with the Sunday school for many years thereafter.

Raking through her nativity box she decided that Michael should go to the Hospital Ball as a Wise Man. She swathed him in satin robes, plonked an ornate turban on his head, did clever things with foil round a teapot to represent the frankincense, and then produced some jesters' shoes with curly points and bells. The final touch was to blacken him.

'Now then, you just get into the car. You'll be a great hit.'

'O-o-oh,' stammered Michael. 'I'm not in the car. I'm on my bike.'

It was with some difficulty that Joan wound his robes around him once he was astride the bike. The frankincense was strapped to the crossbar and off he went. The only trouble was that every time he pedalled the wretched bells on his jesters' shoes went 'tinkle, tinkle'.

As he approached roadworks he saw that the traffic lights were on the blink, so there was a policeman on point duty. As the vision pedalled towards him, the policeman put up his hand to bring him to a halt.

'And where do you think you're going, dressed up like that?' he asked.

To which Michael replied, 'To the mental hospital.'

★ ★ ★

Joan had a lot to account for in our lives. It was she who persuaded us to give a holiday to two brothers from a dysfunctional family from Castleford. Their father was a painter who had fallen off his ladder, broken his leg, and then kicked the mother with his plastered limb. The social worker decided that they might patch up the wonky marriage if they could have some time on their own without their four young children. A worthy charity fixed up a two-week break for their offspring in York. They arrived painted with Gentian violet and bearing nit combs. They had never slept in sheets before, or eaten fresh fruit and vegetables. Joan had the oldest girl, and the youngest boy who, although five, seemed unable to speak. We had the middle two. We took them to Bridlington, but they cried when we took off their shoes and socks on the beach.

'Our mam'd bray us if she knew,' they said.

As we walked along the prom I could feel people staring at us. Michael was wearing his dog collar. I had a little child on each hand, and my bump was obvious. I overheard one woman say to her friend, 'Just look at them – two kids already and her expecting again.' Then they stared in horror as we turned into the amusement arcade and armed our charges with pennies. This was much better than the beach. Maybe we would have to overcome our dislike of slot machines in our mission to give the children a good time at the seaside.

On the last Saturday before they went home we took the four children with us on a Youth Club hike in the Yorkshire Dales. To begin with they ran happily ahead on a path by a stream, but they soon lagged behind. Our younger boy started to cry. Thinking that tiredness was his problem, Michael hoisted him up on his back. It was then that we realised that the cause of his distress was diarrhoea. We washed his offending garments in the stream and made a cloak from the spare anorak I had in my rucksack. The sight of his poor smelly brother led to a torrent of words from the hitherto speechless sibling, who eventually left York for Castleford free of lice and fluent with words!

★ ★ ★

Two weeks before our baby was due I was foolish enough to go with Michael, Joan and our Sunday school to a mammoth Diocesan children's jamboree in the grounds of Bishopthorpe Palace, the residence of the Archbishop of York. York is a huge diocese – so huge that as well as the Archbishop there are suffragan bishops of Hull, Selby and Whitby. Coaches converged on York and disgorged hundreds of excited children who were then herded onto boats to go down the Ouse to Bishopthorpe. Gathering outside the Palace we were greeted by the Diocesan Children's Advisor, and then had a run through some of the songs we were to sing in the afternoon pageant. The most popular one was 'Some folk have to live on a bowl of rice', which went to the tune of 'We all live in a yellow submarine', and was sung with great gusto.

Just as we opened our picnic bags the rain started to drizzle and then to pour. This wonderfully designed day did not have a wet weather option built in to it, and the Archbishop was certainly not going to have hundreds of muddy-footed children romping around his residence. One of our Sunday school teachers came to the rescue. He had run to the village and obtained the keys of the church hall. How I ever got myself and my bump into that hall along with the entire output of York Diocese Sunday school children I shall never know, but I was soon on the stage shouting for order and teaching them the rudiments of 'Do this, do that' – a sort of 'Simon says' game which involved copying my movements. At almost nine months pregnant, agility was not my forte. After ten minutes of putting my arms up and down, standing on one leg, and patting my distended tummy, I was relieved when we were told to leave the hall and proceed to the church in the village.

The pageant had been written with a view to an outdoor performance, with masses of space for processions and banners. How could it possibly be transposed to the confines of pews and narrow aisles? Children sat on the altar steps, the font, with an overflow in the porch. The Diocesan advisor did not know what to advise. In desperation she suggested we greeted the arrival of Archbishop Donald Coggan with a rousing rendition of 'Some folk have to live on a bowl of rice'. He entered fully robed in cope and mitre as the children launched cheerily into 'We all live in a bowl of rice'. He looked bemused.

I sensed that the advisor was mentally planning her letter of resignation.

The next part of the pageant was supposed to make us all aware of how we should try to live the Christian life and the virtues we should aim for. We were also to be aware that the devil would try to stop us and would tempt us with vices. The props included banners bearing seven virtues and seven vices. Middlesbrough were the proud bearers of the virtues and Hull, ensconced in the porch, had to carry the vices. There had, of course, been no rehearsal of the whole pageant and because of the rain there had been no time for a run-through on the day.

Hymns were sung and lessons read. The narrator announced in a dramatic voice, 'And so we must live good lives, and these placards remind us of what we should aim for…'

Before the harassed Middlesbrough Sunday school teachers had marshalled their virtue-bearing scholars, the Hull contingent, thinking this was their cue, swept into church exhorting us to GREED, VANITY, PRIDE and SLOTH. By the time Middlesbrough could issue a counter attack the narrator had already announced, 'And we should never give way to…'

PURITY, PATIENCE, TOLERANCE and LOVE, said the banners from the north.

By this time the Hull children were being marched out to their place in the porch but the Middlesbrough children, tired of being penned in behind the font, followed them out. The remaining children decided that was the end so started to push their way out. The Archbishop looked haggard as he tried to conclude the prematurely ending service in a dignified way, by saying the grace. Not to be outdone the children all started to sing, 'We all live in a bowl of rice.'

He took off his mitre and sadly plodded back to the Palace. The children ran amok and jumped on to the first available boat in the waiting flotilla. No one had any idea which children were on which boat. Back in York we were met by angry cohorts of parents who laid into us for either losing their children, or for doing irreparable damage to their bladders by not having toilet facilities at the Palace. I had little sympathy. I was heavily pregnant and I had managed all right.

'Bye, Miss! Hasn't it been good,' shouted a hefty ginger- haired Middlesbrough girl.

I noted that she was still wafting her banner around. PATIENCE, it said. As I turned round to face the angry mothers I knew I was going to need it. Just then Michael leapt from a following boat, came to my aid and gave my tummy a friendly pat. The mothers' anger miraculously dissipated.

'Maybe we should go and have a Chinese meal,' suggested Michael.

'No thanks', I answered, as I turned homewards singing, 'I don't want to live in a bowl of rice...'

Chapter Three

W e had never had pageants like that in my day, although in the 1940s and 1950s Sunday schools were very much in vogue and invariably met on Sunday afternoons. As a child, in Beverley in the East Riding of Yorkshire, I worked my way up from infants to juniors and seniors, before being prepared for Confirmation. There were 150 of us in St. Nicholas Sunday school, the largest section being the infants whose superintendent was my mother.

Every Sunday, apart from five weeks in the summer, 80 or more three to six-year-olds crammed into the Snooker Institute next to the parish hall. There were only 60 little wooden chairs so the youngest children were lifted up to sit on the edge of the snooker tables. I was under oath not to divulge this to my father who was on the snooker club committee. The tables did have covers over them, and the cues were safely out of reach, but knowing the cost of the tables and re-felting it was somewhat rash to make the thinly veiled green baize the weekly repository for 20 children not long out of nappies.

The juniors met in the parish hall, which always smelt of acrid coke fumes, and were presided over by a fervent lady with hair in a tightly coiled bun. She disciplined us as though we were a pack of unruly dogs. 'SIT!' she barked, and we sat. Maybe Barbara

Woodhouse had learned her techniques in a similar Sunday school. Once 'SAT!' we listened, almost against our will, to riveting stories of Nebuchadnezzar and a dismembered hand writing on the wall, and Delilah sneaking into the tent to cut off Samson's hair. This teacher knew her bible so well and her enthusiasm rubbed off onto all but the naughtiest boys and girls. The hour began and ended with the recitation of that Sunday's Collect, so after four years in the juniors I was very familiar, and in some cases word perfect, with all but the middle Trinity collects which cropped up in August. Such knowledge proved so useful in later years, as did the chunks of scripture we were expected to learn by heart at day school. These, like the 'times tables', chanted in rote have never seeped from my memory.

Enthusiasm for an hour at Sunday school waned as we grew older, but as churchwarden's daughter I was expected to set a good example, and it never occurred to me to put up any resistance. The curate had the dubious privilege of teaching the senior class in church. I don't remember what I learned on Sundays but the Monday evening Lent class left a lasting impression. Only two or three girls ventured out on cold and dark February and March evenings to enter the church, which was lit only by one light bulb and candles in the Sanctuary. It had an eerie, but holy, atmosphere into which entered a young, black-cassocked curate to take us on our weekly spiritual journey on a children's 'Pilgrim's Progress'. Child Protection laws wouldn't allow it today, but our parents never worried about setting us off to walk through the graveyard and into a semi-darkened church to be alone with a young man in his twenties.

We certainly had no fears and returned week after week to catch up with Pilgrim's Progress. So we walked through the wicket-gate, which I always imagined was onto a cricket pitch, past the Slough of Despond, through the Valley of the Shadow of Death and onwards, to arrive in Holy Week at the Celestial City. After each week's instalment, which the curate always left on a cliffhanger, we sat for a few minutes in silence to reflect on the story and how it applied to us. The impact of the story, enhanced by the flickering candlelight and the noise of the wind whistling round the church tower, had a lasting effect on me. I resolved to be Christian's fellow traveller. The hymn we sang every Lent Monday evening was Mrs Alexander's 'Jesus calls us o'er the tumult', with the imploring lines, 'Day by day his sweet voice soundeth, saying, "Christian, follow Me".'

I have an inbuilt resistance to being asked, 'Are you saved?' or 'When would you say you were converted?' For me, the path to Christianity has been an ongoing one, such as Bunyan described, but, as well as my parents, I would have to thank the tightly-bunned teacher for making me 'SIT' for an hour each Sunday afternoon, and the black-cassocked curate, who might have thought his Children's Lent service to be a failure, attracting only three girls. I wonder if the other two girls are still on the pilgrim way. If so, then the curate had a 100% success rate!

Sunday school had its lighter moments. Its parties in January were to be savoured. After the rigours of the war we were certainly ready to party, although party fare was still limited and would sound tame to modern day youth. The mainstay was potted meat sandwiches. Not that the meat came in pots, but in rectangles on greaseproof paper from my Auntie Dora's corner grocery shop. Because my mother was a Sunday school teacher and a member of the Mothers' Union she was one of the kitchen brigade who slaved in a dank church hall kitchen to prepare our tea. Here it was that I learned the quick and economical way of buttering bread. Did I say 'buttering'? Of course I meant 'margarining'. We were still in rationing mode. Blocks of 'marg' were put into a large pan on a low heat to melt. Meanwhile bread was cut into slices and placed in a long line along a trestle table. A paperhanging brush was then plunged into the oily margarine and swept along the awaiting bread slices, in the manner of a watercolour artist administering a background wash. Behind the painter lady came the potted meat purveyor who scraped a less than adequate amount onto alternate slices, and finally came the 'putter on of the tops' and the annual argument of whether it was better to cut them square or diagonal.

We had to eat four quarters of sandwiches before being allowed to progress to the jelly. Sometimes there was blancmange too, with horrid skin that made me retch. With it we were inexplicably made to eat a half slice of bread. Then came jam tarts and slab cake – this being a bright yellow, closely grained cake with no cream or icing, and usually rather dry. To swill it down there was no orange juice. Children were expected to drink tea, which was poured from huge brown enamel teapots by huge grey godly matrons. At one party we had sugar lumps instead of ordinary sugar. This was a novelty. I have a sweet tooth and gingerly put in three lumps. A boy who had the unfortunate name of Christopher Rump was seen to put twelve in his tea, and was subsequently banished into the church hall porch for the duration of the film show during which we had 'to let our stomachs settle'.

A thin man with spectacles took ages to set up his projector. The blurred films were jerky black and white ones involving gangsters and car chases, but the highlight was when the film snapped, or on one occasion when the whole thing caught on fire. The smell of burning celluloid was nearly as bad as the coke fire.

Sometimes we had a Mr Palmer who brought his Punch and Judy show. Politically incorrect though it may be nowadays, we loved the authoritarian Mr Punch, the voracious crocodile, the strings of sausages and the hard-hitting truncheon of the Bobby. Then we had party games. Some I hated – especially those that involved bursting balloons. Others I loved, especially blindman's buff, which had been suitably adapted for little Christians. One boy was blindfolded and put in the centre of the circle. He was to be 'Jacob'. One of the girls was chosen to be 'Rachel'. Jacob would then call out in Shakespearean tones, 'Rachel, Rachel, wherefore art thou, Rachel?' To which Rachel would reply, 'Here am I, Jacob.' Jacob would then run to where he thought she was (though of course she had now run to another part of the circle) and he would kiss the girl he thought was Rachel. I can't think how the game ever ended. Maybe it hinged on whether Jacob was an attractive boy and was therefore in demand. Or maybe the godly matrons saw it getting out of hand and substituted 'passing the parcel' or 'musical chairs'.

The party ended with prize-giving. We were always given books which, in immediate post-war Britain, were very popular. The value of the book was determined in strict proportion to the attendance you had achieved at Sunday school during the preceding year. This was checked out by the number of adhesive sticky stamps in your stamp book. Each Sunday you were given a stamp, marked Epiphany 1 or Lent 3 to stick in a marked square in a poorly stapled little book. As the party grew nearer there was a black market in stamps. One boy who had left Sunday school, but who had half a book of stamps, swapped his now useless stamps for a liquorice stick and a penny sherbet.

I had to stay to the bitter end of the party, helping mother to take down trestle tables and fold the sheets that had acted as tablecloths. We picked up the puckered burst balloons, swept the hall out with two-foot yard brushes so that the hall would be ready for next day's Sunday school. We usually had an egg for breakfast on Sundays – but never on the Sunday after the party. What do you think went into the frying pan? Bacon? Oh no. Into the sizzling fat went the leftover dry, curled up potted meat sandwiches. Their Resurrection Day had arrived!

Chapter Four

The thought of those fried-up potted meat sandwiches would have turned my stomach in my pregnant York days. I was in danger of hitting anyone who said, 'It will all pass in three months, dear.' Not until month eight did I gain any respite from my sickness. Then, one Sunday, feeling human at last, I leapt out of bed and cooked bacon and egg for Michael, his necessary fuel for a round of services. That day he was on duty at the parish church but I walked from our red brick semi, through the housing estate to the mission church – a temporary building on the very edge of York.

The senior curate was taking the service. Walter was a pleasant man – his landlady's pride and joy. Unlike Michael he never had a hair out of place. I used to wish that one day he would have his cassock buttoned up all wrong. But he never did. I looked at his crisp surplice and gave credit to his landlady for her laundering skills. There again, she wasn't tired and pregnant, and she probably had an ironing board. I had to manage with a folded blanket on the kitchen table, and a succession of damp hankies to make some steam. I tried turning my thoughts to more spiritual things, but the room was airless and oppressive. I was glad when it was time to move and go up for communion. No sooner had I received it and gone back to my place than I was transported to another sphere.

I was lying on cool dewy grass beneath a turquoise sky with celestial music surrounding me. A thoughtful person gave me a pillow and someone threw a coat over me. That was nice. So was the glass of water. I closed my eyes, still wondering where I was. When I opened them there was no doubt. I was in heaven. I recognised the music – 'Jesu, joy of man's desiring' - and then I saw Him, dressed like an angel in white apparel with wide flowing sleeves which He wafted over my face.

I was surprised that He looked so worried. I was even more surprised to see that He was wearing shiny black shoes and had trousers on underneath His angelic garb. He knelt down beside me, not at all sure what to do, but the bystanders were shouting instructions. 'Leave her to us, Walter. You just cycle down to the parish church and tell Michael that his wife has fainted, but that she's all right.'

I was cosseted by everyone in that ninth month. Well, by almost everyone. Michael's treat for me was a day trip by train to the Solway Firth, via the Pennines, traversing Shap on the way out and Ais Gill on the way back. We were hauled by a Merchant Navy Class 'United States Line', by 'Gordon Highlander' and by '123', which I know will impress any steam enthusiasts. On the West Cumbria coast we rattled up lines long since closed to passenger traffic. At the end of each little branch line the other three or four hundred passengers leapt off, cameras slung over their duffel coats, to capture such rare mileage on film. I stood alone, or should I say with my bump, in the open doorway of the train – too large and cumbersome to jump down onto the track. In later years I saw slides and ciné films of this momentous steam excursion, and proudly pointed to the turquoise blob protruding from the carriage door.

Despite sweating through a very hot July I was relieved that the baby did not come prematurely. Our wedding had been at the end of October. I could imagine what the godly matrons of the parish would be thinking if I gave birth in mid-July, and could visualise them counting up on their fingers and tut-tutting. Three days after the expected delivery date, I relaxed.

The Mothers' Union met on a Tuesday night in the mission hut. I declined attending their July meeting as my back was aching and I didn't want to sit on a wooden chair, or risk fainting again. The vicar's wife said that they would say a prayer for me. That obviously did the trick, for within an hour I had sent for the midwife, a competent middle-aged lady who exuded confidence. She was an ardent Roman Catholic and engaged Michael in theological debate most of the night, in between drinking tea and keeping an eye on me. I duly contracted, inhaled gas and air, panted and eventually pushed. At 7.15 a.m. our little boy was born, weighing in at 8 lbs. We had drawn up a shortlist of names (with Stephen reserved as a second name, of course) and reeled these off before the midwife left. There was no doubt in her mind as to what he should be called. She pointed to a black and gold picture of St. Christopher on the bedroom wall and announced, 'He should be Christopher – patron saint of travellers.' That was settled then!

Michael had to be at church at 8 a.m. for the daily Matins service. He had no time to waste so he rushed down to telephone our parents.

'Just one boy,' he said.

I did not like his use of the word 'just'. How many had he expected me to produce? I had given every ounce of strength to producing his son and heir. He leapt onto his bike and I heard him shout to the neighbours, 'Just one boy! I think that Margaret might like some breakfast.'

Margaret certainly did. Mrs Henderson from across the road obliged with two rounds of toast and mountains of fluffy yellow scrambled egg. Heedless of the midwife's parting advice – 'now don't be in a hurry to eat; you've had quite a bit of gas and air' – I seized on the breakfast like a starved castaway on a desert island. Despite its inevitable return journey that scrambled egg still rates as the most enjoyable meal of my life.

The rest of the day was a euphoric mix of congratulatory grandparents and parishioners, and some heavenly naps. Michael looked suitably impressed with his 'just one son' but he had other things on his mind. Urgently. The following day he had to sit his Priests' Exam. He would have to burn the midnight oil. Keeping awake was no problem. Christopher saw to that. After two nights with no sleep Michael was not in the best physical or mental state to sit an exam, but he passed, and two months later the Archbishop of York, Dr Donald Coggan ordained him priest in York Minster in the morning and christened Christopher at our parish church in the afternoon. Showing exemplary Yorkshire economy we had arranged it this way so that our relatives and friends would have to make only one journey, and we would have to give them only one meal, sandwiched between the two services.

The Archbishop next saw Christopher sandwiched between the revolving doors of the Esplanade Hotel in Scarborough the following spring. Michael was at a clergy school, paid for by the diocese, and wives and children were invited too. Christopher by now was adept at manipulating his baby-walking frame, in which he scuttled around, crashing into low-lying coffee tables in pursuit of the nuts and crisps lying tantalisingly in little bowls.

I was in an animated conversation with another curate's wife, sympathising with her on having a fiendish vicar and wife in comparison with our caring and helpful couple, when I heard a loud hammering by the entrance. Three sections of the revolving door were filled with desperate members of the Church of England's hierarchy banging on the glass and pointing to an apparently empty section. I ran to their aid, casting an eye out to see where Christopher was. He was not in the lounge. Living up to his name he had travelled to see what was in the big, wide world outside and found himself and his baby-walking frame caught up in moving apparatus. The more frantic the trapped clergy became, the more wedged became the frame. I wickedly wished that I had my camera to capture the scene. Which caption would be better? 'Church of England locked in debate' or 'Anglican church going round in circles'? I knocked on the glass of the door loudly, causing Christopher to jerk in my direction. With his wheels realigned I coaxed him with a dish of crisps so that he would pedal himself round in the right direction, and thereby release the honoured clerical guests who were due to give the 11 a.m. lecture. I doubted whether the diocese would consider inviting wives and children to their next conference.

Surprisingly they did. The following June we were all invited to Butlin's holiday camp in Filey. Michael and I arrived in casual summer clothes but were in the minority. As we walked to our chalet we were passed by a jolly engine trailing open carriages in which sat most of the York diocese delegates, all in black suits or cassocks, with briefcases and rolled umbrellas. The 'men from the ministry' were on route to their chalets. Their grim expressions gave the impression that they were not going to enjoy the holiday camp experience. We had decided that we would. In our free time we mingled with 'normal' holidaymakers, sampled the ice cream and candy floss, peered in at knobbly knee and glamorous grandma competitions, and toured the funfair. One afternoon we joined in a sports event. Michael, who had been captain of the harriers at university, fancied his chances in one of the races and duly crashed through the finishing tape in first place. The organisers were mystified by this unregistered tape-crasher; all other competitors were bearing the colours of their 'houses'. However they gave him a prize – a large box of after-shave products - and the announcer called for a round of applause for 'the sporting vicar'.

While the delegates were embroiled in high-powered theological seminars and discussions, I made use of the baby-minding service and went for a swim in the new pool, which had glass sides. Every time we had walked through the passageway to the dining hall we had stopped to look through the glass at the swimmers and divers who appeared like fishes in a giant aquarium. Now I was keen to see it from the inside. After half an hour of swimming I thought I would do one dive before lunch. I was wearing a new swimming costume; it was soon to fail its first test, for as I dived, the force of the water filled the cups and dragged the costume down. Now bare-breasted I panicked and swam underwater to the nearest wall, where I could make myself more decent before popping above the water line. I chose the wall unwisely. It was the glass one by the passageway through which were passing the clergy of the York diocese, newly disgorged from their seminar. Fifty pairs of incredulous clerical eyes watched as I sorted out my cups and straps. Forty years on I am sure they have forgotten everything in that seminar but will still remember everything in that passageway!

We returned home with one swimming costume in need of strap reorientation, one box of aftershave lotion and a serious matter for discussion some two months later:

Having given Christopher the second name of Stephen, after his place of conception, would we really be happy to call our second baby Billy? Butlin's had a lot to answer for!

Chapter Five

While we were pondering names for baby number two, the good ladies of the parish took to their knitting needles again, regardless of the fact that of the 58 cardigans and matinée coats they had made for Christopher we still had 30 unused ones. I then had to break it to the Mothers' Union and Ladies Fellowship that I wasn't even going to have the baby in their parish – we were on the move to a second curacy in the dockland area of Hull.

Michael decided we should temper the trauma of a house move by packing up, and then going away on holiday, to return rejuvenated for the actual move and the unpacking. I was by now at the height, or I would say depth, of my all-day sickness. A hotel was out of the question; a curate's stipend did not stretch to that. But we could afford a railway camping coach, if we invited others to join us. And so, in the September of 1967 my student cousin, Dudley, Michael's Auntie Win, and her friend Lucy, joined us for a week in Arisaig on the west coast of Scotland.

One condition of the camping coach holiday was that we had to travel by rail. This was an added attraction for Michael, and I must admit it was a thrill to stand on platform 9 of York Station, awaiting the sleeper train to Fort William. I gazed across fondly at platform 8 South where, five years earlier, Michael had popped on my engagement ring. Then I was a single young lady working as a medical social worker in Sheffield and living in an attic flat. Now I was a curate's wife, mother of one and a bit and about to move house again.

The train roared in, breaking my reverie, and we were soon installed in our compartment, speeding up the East Coast main line. I snuggled down into the crisp white sheets and grey blanket, with the attendant's promise ringing in my ears: 'The next thing you'll hear is me knocking at the door and bringing you a cup of tea as we pass through Crianlarich.'

That was not the case. The next thing I heard was the sound of the blind being pulled up and Michael saying, 'Margaret – look out – we're just passing Durham Cathedral.' Then, at increasingly frequent intervals, 'I think we're waiting for the signal,' and 'Don't miss the sight of the moon on the sea' and other injunctions. His railway adrenalin was flowing fast. So was my sickness. Eventually I felt more comfortable and managed to nod off. Guess where? On the approach to Crianlarich!

The Pullman coach at Arisaig was beautifully situated and I was impressed by its size. It was far bigger than the biggest caravan I had ever been in. It had a well-equipped kitchen, a large lounge/dining area, three bedrooms, and an open area at each end. But where was the toilet? Perusal of the 'notes for happy campers' revealed that we were to use the toilet on the station platform. I could foresee a penny shortage by the end of the day, so sent the others off into the village to accumulate a good supply, while wondering if it would be robbing the railways of vital revenue if we held the door open for each other. My worries were in vain. The stationmaster came across the line bearing two precious keys with which we could bypass the slot mechanism.

It was a glorious September. We bathed, lay on the white sands of Morar and did healthy walks. We also tried out our new camera. The standard 8 ciné camera had film that had to be changed over halfway. Unknown to Michael I had already used one side and changed onto side two. He then filmed to the end of that side and duly changed it round again for scenic shots in the heather, finishing the film off at a Yorkshire safari park. Most people nod off to sleep when subjected to other people's holiday films. Not our audience. They were entranced with breathtaking shots of elephants walking through the heather, giraffes standing in Scottish lochs and rhinos paddling in the sea.

'How on earth did you get those special effects?' they asked.

'All a matter of teamwork,' we answered, quite truthfully.

North-west Scotland one week. East Riding of Yorkshire the next. Our furniture, which had filled our York semi-detached house, seemed rather sparse in the large Edwardian vicarage in Hull, which we inhabited as the vicar was a bachelor and preferred to live in the curate's house. The words, 'The Lord will provide' had been firmly entrenched in my mind. The Lord duly sent relatives, friends and parishioners to the rescue, with second-hand sofas, curtains and carpets. Before I grew any larger I set to with paintbrush and floor stain. My mother-in-law who, in her time, had needed a cheap way of dealing with acres of vicarage floors, recommended permanganate of potash. This looked alarmingly purple when mixed, but it stained all our bedroom floors and dried to a pleasant dark brown. My one winter maternity outfit was also brown. As I let out the waist tapes bit by bit so I let out my loathing of this brown bouclé suit. As February gave way to March and my expected date of delivery slipped into the past, I resolved that the first thing I would do after giving birth would be to burn the offending garment.

Meanwhile we had to discuss baby names. Despite our baby's Butlin's conception we ruled out Billy. Just as well, as I gave birth to a girl. We called her Pauline. The root of that name comes from the Latin for little. Little she was not. The midwife glowed in the approbation of the GP who commended her on delivering, single-handed and with no stitching needed, a ten-and-a-half-pound baby.

After two days of continuous visitors the doctor advised undisturbed rest. Michael went out – on a parish visit, I presumed - or was it to escape from the wrath of his Auntie Win who had been imported to help during the confinement? She had envisaged the descent of visitors who might need feeding so had made a huge trifle. We didn't possess or need a fridge in a non-centrally heated house, so we used to put excess food into the oven, away from the mice who were frequent visitors. When parents-in-law and aunts and uncles arrived for baby viewing, Auntie proudly offered them trifle, but was horrified at finding the large glass trifle bowl, which resided in the oven, empty apart from an incriminating spoon. Mice don't usually use spoons! When challenged, Michael said casually, 'Oh, I was hungry after the council meeting, so I looked in the oven to see what I could eat, and I just tidied it up.'

The next thing I heard was Auntie, with Christopher in his pushchair, stomping down the gravel drive of the vicarage, muttering, 'Just tidied it up, indeed.' Michael was next out of the house, so I took the opportunity to feed Pauline and curl up for a much-needed rest. I was just dozing off when an earthquake struck. Clank, bang, judder; the house shook. I leapt to the window and looked out to see Michael and fellow curate David wielding drills and hammers, to add some unusual décor to the front of the vicarage.

It was a smoke box door. Do you know what that is? Neither did the scrap metal dealer who was cutting up redundant steam engines in a Hull scrapyard. When Michael had asked, 'What are the chances of my getting a smoke box door?' he had replied, 'No problem – I'll get one of my men to deliver one.'

Later, when he had seen his men struggling to load up on a lorry the whole front of an engine, he realised what a smoke box door was, but to his credit would not go back on his promise to a man of the cloth.

It was delivered on a Saturday afternoon just as Michael was about to go over to church to officiate at a wedding. Seeing the lorry coming down Church Lane he leapt into his navy boiler suit, donned a black beret and ran to help the men unload the precious cargo. By this time I could see the bridesmaids' car arriving at the church. It was only when I saw the bride's mother step out of her car with stiletto heels, chiffon frock and picture hat, that I panicked. So did she. Was that oily, dishevelled, boiler-suited young man that she had just passed really the same freshly scrubbed curate she had shaken hands with only yesterday when she had come to supervise the floral arrangements in church? Just in time, before the bridal car swept up the lane, Michael stepped out of his working gear, applied Swarfega to his hands, and appeared in spotless white surplice in the porch, with half a minute to spare, to greet the bride and her father.

I don't remember Michael asking the vicar's permission to adorn our home with such a huge railway relic. I doubt if he could have counteracted the enthusiasm of his two rail-mad curates who, as Auntie Win returned from her walk, were adding the final touch of a railway lamp onto the smoke box door bracket. My post-natal rest had been abandoned; I leant out of the bedroom window and shouted, 'How about a celebration party? I think Auntie Win has made a large trifle.'

Another trifle had to be made three weeks later. Pauline was growing so fast that if we delayed her baptism any longer, she wouldn't fit into the family heirloom Victorian christening gown. With a preponderance of clergy wishing to participate, it was a job to apportion jobs for them all. In the end Michael's Uncle Tom did the churching, Michael baptised, the vicar and curate shared the prayers, and Grandpa gave the blessing. Our previous vicar said grace before a buffet meal. I served the trifle. We lined up on the lawn for a family photo, with the cranes from King George dock in the background. The outgoing Rotterdam ferry hooted its congratulations.

Ships' hoots were a source of great concern to Winnie, our elderly organist, especially on Sunday mornings and evenings. Michael has a good, rich voice, but it doesn't know when or where to hover on the requisite note for the versicles in Morning and Evening Prayer. Only after many years' practice was he able to home in on a bottom G. In Hull his pitch difficulties were compounded when services coincided with high tide, for he was more likely to take his note from the hoot of the outgoing ship than from the note that Winnie was patiently hammering out. If it was a little ship, then the resultant note was a high falsetto, uttering, 'O Lord, open thou our lips.' Conversely, if it was a big ship, then Michael's note plummeted to a deep bass, an octave and several semi or quarter tones lower than Winnie's note.

Despite her problems with the curate's wandering voice, Winnie bore no grudges, which was just as well, as one Sunday night she finished up in an adjacent bed to Michael, albeit in the accident and emergency ward of Hull Infirmary. They had been together at evensong. I was at home putting Christopher and Pauline to bed. At half past seven Michael burst into the vicarage, sat on the stool by the phone in the hall, and started dialling. In the middle of doing so he fell off. Thinking he was acting the fool I lifted him back up and told him not to be so silly. He slumped again. Before I could act, the wardens were at the door sprinting to the phone to dial 999. Apparently it was not only Michael who was in a state of collapse, but several members of the choir and congregation too.

Soon the large vicarage hall was full of bodies. Some groaned, some were sick, and they all looked grey. The emergency services were quick to arrive and a fleet of ambulances whisked away the casualties, while the fire service investigated the cause. The chief fireman was dubious about the source of the poisonous fumes that had been leaking into church. He opened the boiler house door and then he believed. Reeling like a drunken man he had to agree with the theory that work in conjunction with the making of the new docks must have disrupted the pipes of the church boiler, causing a lethal seepage of carbon monoxide. This had affected everyone in the chancel and the front of the church, and had hit Michael and Winnie the hardest.

Michael was discharged later that night and told to take things easy the next day. That was easier said than done, for in the early hours of the morning the phone went. It was Hull Maternity Hospital wanting Michael to perform an emergency baptism on a newborn baby. Having been a premature baby himself, needing to be baptised straight away, he was always especially prompt in dealing with such emergencies. The taxi outside was hooting as I watched, bemused, as Michael put on his trousers on top of his pyjamas. Was that for speed or was he still hazy after his gassing? I often wondered if that tiny baby survived; if so then he or she would never know that the baptiser was a woozy curate complete with pyjama bottoms.

Splashed on the Monday edition of the Hull Daily Mail was an account of the 'Evensong Gassing', complete with photo of curate Michael and organist Winnie. It was one of the most exciting episodes of her life, and her conversations in her last years were interspersed with, 'Did you know I was once in the next bed to the curate?'

On our next holiday, a much younger lady, Carol, was to have that privilege too.

Chapter Six

On our Scottish holiday films the elephants in the heather at our Arisaig camping coach were followed by nappies and bras on a line strung across the railway line in Stromeferry. Friends from our York days joined us on our second camping coach holiday on the Inverness to Kyle of Lochalsh line. There was no public transport to this coach – only the ferry or the railway. We gave our shopping list to the guard of the morning train into Kyle and he would deliver our goods on his return trip. I bet he had never had to shop for a baby's dummy before! Pauline was not quite three months old and was still demanding an early morning feed. Her cries were greeted initially with my, 'Oh please go back to sleep again, I'm on holiday and I'm tired.' But the breathtaking sight of a June dawn across Loch Carron made this early morning feed almost a pleasure. As I nursed my hungry daughter I sang an introit I had learned at school: 'High o'er the lonely hills, black turns to grey; birdsong the valley fills, mists roll away. Grey wakes to green again, beauty is seen again; gold and serene again dawns the new day.' When the rest of the family and friends eventually awoke for breakfast at 8 a.m. I was unbearably smug.

'You should really get up at 4.30 a.m. and watch the sun rise. I do it every day.'

The temporary washing line was strung across the track once the morning train had gone back to Inverness. Wherever we walked during the day we had to have frequent time checks to ensure we were back before the afternoon train rounded the far bends of the loch. When it hooted its imminent arrival I would rush out, unpeg our laundry, unhook the washing line and stand at the trackside with my pile of dazzling nappies, nursing bras and nighties and wave to the driver.

★ ★ ★

The following year we gave our camping coach allegiance to Wales rather than Scotland. Michael had been at college in Lampeter and had fallen in love with Wales immediately, so he was keen to return. The other reason was that the fare was much cheaper. Our large vicarage was close to the Humber, with east winds that blew unbroken from Russia, and we were trying to remain solvent on an income of £500 a year to feed and clothe a family of four. With true Yorkshire economy we invited friends, Carol, Maurice and four-year-old Warren, from our previous parish in York to join us, in the full knowledge that Maurice worked for the railways and would be able to get the camping coach at an even more advantageous rate than we would. We also chose to holiday in early October, which was extremely off-peak, and so whittled the price down to £9 for the week.

At the last minute Maurice found he was unable to take the time off, but Carol and Warren joined us as planned and we all travelled by rail to Aberdyfi on the Cardigan coast. We had good weather and enjoyed bracing walks, played hide-and-seek in the dunes, dreamed up inventive menus, played snap and housey-housey after tea, and indulged in early nights. One afternoon we had over-enthusiastically walked along a rocky path to Picnic Island and beyond. Pauline's pushchair was squeaking and groaning about its lack of oil and abundance of sand, and the two little boys were groaning about the long trek back. We placated them by promising orange squash at the first café we could find. The autumn wind was blowing in our faces and we adults urgently needed to get in somewhere warm and have a hot drink. Cafés that are open in October in the environs of a small Welsh seaside town proved non-existent. In the distance we saw a sandwich board propped outside a hall. My spirits rose as I was sure it was the Mothers' Union or Women's Institute holding an afternoon tea. My saliva was already forming at the prospect of Welsh cakes and bara brîth to accompany the much longed-for tea.

Disappointment set in as we drew nearer and saw that the Aberdyfi Reading Room was the venue, not for a tea party, but for a blood donation session. Undaunted, Michael marched us all in and ordered Carol and me to get out our blood donation cards. He reckoned that if we all gave blood, then we would qualify for a free cup of tea. He assumed that the kind WRVS ladies would have pity on the boys and give them some orange squash and a biscuit.

I was not allowed to give blood; it was too soon after giving birth, so I sat in the waiting area, thankfully being warmed up by a complimentary cup of tea. Michael and Carol stretched out on beds, hands around little wooden sticks, clenching and unclenching, as their precious blood dripped into plastic bags. Suddenly I heard voices. The nurse was shouting to Michael, 'I'm afraid your wife has passed out.'

Michael's indignant reply was, 'She's not my wife, she's the lady I'm on holiday with.'

The WRVS lady, brandishing the teapot, almost dropped it in horror. She had noted on Michael's card that he was a Reverend. She was the local minister's wife. I had much explaining to do in order to put the record straight.

Carol regained consciousness, enjoyed a cup of tea and was driven back to the camping coach by the minister's wife, who called round the next day to enquire about her health. Carol was suffering from a tummy bug so spent the next two days in bed, her recovery aided by visits from her Welsh ministering angel bearing medication and culinary delicacies for weak stomachs. Carol returned to York to regale the parish, and her husband, with tales to outdo those that Winnie was trumpeting in Hull about being in the next bed to the vicar. It was time for us to return home and try to establish some normality.

★ ★ ★

Our dockland parish was enormous in both area and population, and the workload for vicar and curates was similarly large. We were close to the Hull prison, and had in our parish the maternity hospital and the Missions to Seamen's institute. As well as the normal Sunday services in four churches, and the vast number of baptisms, weddings and funerals, there were Scouts and Guides, Brownies and Cubs, Ladies Fellowships, Mothers' Unions, Sunday schools and youth clubs. The youth club from St. Giles church met in the Church Institute across the road from the vicarage. Around it was set an array of industries – Fenners Industrial belts, Priestmans cranes, Imperial typewriters, Seven Seas cod liver oil, and Humbrol paints factories.

One Guy Fawkes Day Humbrol paints almost ceased to exist. Michael and the youth club had decided to hold a big bonfire and firework party on the grass outside the institute. To their credit they had asked Humbrol if this was acceptable, and were told that unless the wind was in a certain direction they could go ahead. On the night everything seemed to be fine, Humbrol gave their approval and the fire was lit. Having put Pauline to bed, I took Christopher into the front bedroom of the vicarage to watch the firework display. The bonfire was going well and I could see silhouetted figures plying it with planks and old pallets. Sparks went ever higher, and as they rose they changed direction - the direction of the paint factory. There was obviously an air current at a higher level, on which we had not bargained. A very anxious Michael ran over to

Humbrol, who had posted men on their roof ready for emergency action. He then ran back and instructed the youth club to stop priming the fire and to put it out as fast as they could. I did not move from my position by the vicarage bedroom window until the last spark had settled and the future of both Humbrol and my husband's position as a Church of England curate were ensured.

In the New Year our thoughts turned to holidays. What could we afford? The cheapest thing would be to camp. We had tried this on a two-day break near Shap. Michael and I slept in the tiny one-man tent he had bought when a teenager, and our toddler son and baby daughter slept in a borrowed tent adjacent to ours. At the time we didn't feel as though we were naïve or irresponsible parents. Now, if our children let our grandchildren sleep alone, we would be horrified.

To say that we slept at all on that camping holiday would be to stretch the truth. The tents were pitched extremely close to the Scout Green signal box and my slumber attempts were punctuated by Michael sticking his head under the canvas to view the engine labouring up the bank, and to count the number of wagons, and then to get the number of the banking engine at the rear. In less than half an hour the banking engine would return and out would pop Michael's head again. There was no respite between trains, as a group of desperate enthusiasts recorded, on an ancient tape-recorder, every engine's laboured progress up Shap and played it back at full volume. I tossed and turned and wondered if this constituted mental cruelty and grounds for divorce. The alternative would be to buy a bigger tent in which we could all sleep and which would be too big to be erected on the narrow strip of grass next to that railway line.

Having decided on the alternative I now had to devise a way of earning some income. A letter arrived from York. It was from Joan, our Sunday school teacher friend. She too had wanted some extra cash and had responded to an advert in the local paper from Sadler's Wells Ballet wanting accommodation for members of their company while performing in the city. Having three daughters who fancied themselves as ballerinas, Joan thought how splendid it would be to have three dancers to stay for the week. She responded to the advert. The girls rushed to the door when they heard the taxi arrive. They expected to greet Giselle, the Sleeping Beauty and a Swan. On the doorstep stood three hefty technicians, and not a tutu in sight.

I was therefore well forewarned of the possible outcome when I replied to the Hull Mail advert for accommodation for members of the Sadler's Wells Opera Company. I fully expected two electricians or stagehands. When two attractive lady opera stars arrived my cup of happiness was full. Michael's was overflowing! They stayed for ten days in an April that contained no showers, but gave us day after day of warm sunshine. I cooked them breakfast and an evening meal, which they said tasted so much nicer in a proper home rather than in a sterile hotel. In the mornings they went over to the church institute to 'open their throats' and in the afternoons they invited various groups of friends from the opera company to sample 'tea on the vicarage lawn'. I wafted around with plates of cucumber sandwiches, the children had masses of attention, and Michael arranged tours of the docks for the men.

Our two guests were in a state of high excitement. For the younger one, from New Zealand, it was her first tour and she was in the chorus of Die Fledermaus. The older one was singing her first solo part in La Traviata. We were given complimentary tickets for one show; we chose Die Fledermaus. At the end of their memorable stay our delightful guests presented us with a long-playing record of that opera, signed on the sleeve. We often wonder how their careers progressed, but have no record of their real names, for they had signed themselves using the names that three-year-old Christopher had given them: 'Trevor Arta and Freda Mouse,'

As well as this record, which we still possess, we received enough money to buy a second-hand frame tent. It was time to go away with the vicar once more.

Chapter Seven

The orange tent canvas, which had lain like a stranded whale on the vicarage lawn, suddenly billowed outwards and upwards in a bid to blow into the more affluent west end of Hull. Michael stymied its escape and anchored it down with a wheelbarrow and a child, then joined me in trying to solve the pole-matching puzzle that seemed to demand an IQ of considerably more points than we had inherited. The original markings on the junction of each pole had disappeared. The previous owners had lost the instruction book. It was a mistake to start our trial tent-pitching after tea. The children were tired and fractious and darkness was descending fast. Two hours and a new torch battery later we stood back to admire our new holiday home; the owl in the ash tree hooted his approval.

Flushed with success we proceeded to dismantle the poles in readiness for the next test – 'spatial awareness'. In other words, could we fit the canvas and poles back neatly into the awaiting bags? Only when we had pulled apart the door canopy section did we think that it would have been a good idea to make our own colour coding of which pole fitted into which. Half an hour later, having re-erected the canopy and stuck onto the pole ends varying numbers of insulating tape rings, we could strike camp. Of course we couldn't fit the amorphous bulk of canvas into the ridiculously small bag. Our blood sugar levels were low; I had tripped over a vicious tent peg in the dark; blood trickled from my leg and I was already resenting the hard-earned £15 we had forked out for the tent.

'It's a silly idea to think of camping with two small children,' I muttered, as I dragged my weary feet up the oak staircase of the vicarage. 'I'd have been quite happy to have gone on day trips to Hornsea.'

'Whose idea was it to get a tent?' countered Michael. 'You've gone on and on about your wonderful camping holidays with the Guides.'

It was true. Was I looking back at those days with rose-coloured spectacles? Or were the old-fashioned Girl Guide bell tents with only one solid wooden pole far easier to erect than the modern frame tents?

My love affair with camping, hiking, tracking and knotting began in the Brownies. When I was six I put on a shapeless brown cotton dress, pinched in by a belt, learned to turn a yellow triangle into something resembling a tie, secured it round my neck with a right over left and left over right reef knot so it would stay flat, and finished off my ensemble with a brown woolly hat with a large bobble. Which 'six' would I be placed in? Would I be one of the Pixies, who went round 'helping others when in fixes'? Or one of the Elves, who were into 'helping others not themselves'? Of course, I could have been put in the sprightly Sprites. I can't remember what they did. Maybe I should concoct an advert:

'Calling any Brownie Sprites. Please let me know if you are flying kites, avoiding fights, or knitting tights.'

Obviously Baden-Powell's poetic skills were on the wane when he, or more likely his sister Agnes or wife Olave, came to write the rhyming couplet for the 'six' that was about to be augmented by little Margaret Jefferson. Joining hands in a circle we skipped round singing, 'Here we are the Little People, aim as high as any steeple.' I must admit I can't come up with any other rhyme for people, and in retrospect think the aim was rather fitting for a future vicar's wife!

I loved Brownies. I coloured in flags, learned how to set a table for the dinner parties we never had, and how to make a sling from an unfolded Brownie tie. The only thing with which I had difficulty was achieving the necessary number of ticks for the Health card. No, I don't mean blood-sucking arachnids, of which I am sure there were plenty in the ancient feather bed which I shared with my sister. I refer to the pencil ticks on the card to show that I was a clean and hygienic Brownie. Baden-Powell decreed that it was unhealthy to sleep with a vest on. Baden-Powell had not had to suffer the 1947 winter in a corner terraced house facing north-east, and with only one small fire. For the sake of that vital tick I endured a month of cold non-vest nights. I prayed that my older sister would decide on an early night, so that I could snuggle up to her in our double bed and raise my body temperature to normal.

Then there was the question of teeth cleaning. I could tick the box only if I could swear (on Brownie honour) that I had cleaned my teeth twice a day. Hitherto I had not cleaned my teeth at all. I was born to elderly parents who already had false teeth, which received their daily cleaning in a large tumbler of water on the front bedroom mantelpiece. Dental hygiene for their little girl was non-existent. What should I do? Baden-Powell came to my rescue. Following his instructions I found a stick, whittled off the bark at one end, and splayed out the fibres to make a rough brush. I then dipped this into salt and brushed my little teeth vigorously. It probably ruined the enamel, but it gained me a tick and a Health badge.

From Brownies I flew up into Guides, where I was put into the Poppy patrol. Thank goodness we didn't have any rhyming couplets to endure. I had no desire to be floppy, soppy or stroppy. I loved Guides even more than Brownies, and spent happy Tuesday evenings going out tracking, playing team games and singing jolly songs. Many of the skills I acquired now seem archaic. Mobile phones have put an end to my dream of rescuing a badly injured climber by using my perfect semaphore or Morse abilities to signal SOS. Yet I still thank Guides for teaching me how to knot. In my fifties I even bought advanced knotting books and learned macramé.

Guide knot number one was, of course, the reef knot – not to be undertaken by grannies! However, if ropes were of different thickness you had to make a loop with the thick piece, pop the bunny up through the hole and round the tree and back with the thin piece, and produce a non-slip sheet bend. For tying jam-jars for grandchildren to go tadpole catching, or to lift up your steamed suet puddings, it is essential to have been a Guide or Scout and know how to do a fisherman's knot. And only recently did I bring out my pièce de résistance to shorten my son's dangling cords on his window blinds which now proudly display my perfectly executed sheepshanks.

Deprived of my chance to rescue injured climbers from mountains using my semaphore skills I did keep up with practising the ultimate rescue knot – the bowline on a bight.

I was therefore looking forward to displaying this skill many years later in Michael's last parish, on Sea Sunday. The sermon was based on the theme of rescue from drowning. God is always there to rescue us and to throw out the lifeline when we are floundering. To illustrate this, churchwarden Ray, a retired sea captain, threw out a rope from the pulpit. I was summoned from the congregation to be rescued. He had produced a bowline on a bight with two loops. One went round my middle and the other under my bottom.

Had I known that I was to be a stooge, rather than a knot-demonstrator, I would have taken the precaution of wearing trousers. As it happened I was wearing my 'Sea Sunday outfit' consisting of a silky navy suit emblazoned with anchors and sailing ships. The congregation certainly remembered that sermon.

Maybe they clung on to the idea of God rescuing them, as I clung on to that rope which was inexorably pulling me halfway up the pulpit side. But I rather fear that their memories will forever be of their vicar's wife with skirt pulled up to her waistline revealing more than was fitting in a Welsh church on a Sunday morning. Perhaps I should have been one of those sprightly Sprites, for then I would have been sure of wearing tights. No such luck. I was wearing suspenders and stockings!

Chapter Eight

'To camp, or not camp?' That was the question when we had eventually shoved our unfolded tent into its seam-splitting bag and dressed my tent-peg-punctured leg. We tossed and turned that night and wondered how we would tell the children that camping holidays were 'on hold'. A letter, which arrived the next morning, instantly solved that problem. It was from my university friend, Daphne, who had recently been widowed. She had a toddler son and a baby daughter and a very large frame tent that she was unable to put up on her own. So it was that we agreed to camp together.

'We'll help you to put up your tent,' we said, in an early morning rush of confidence about our pole-assembly skills. 'Maybe we could use part of your large tent as our joint kitchen area.'

As both Daphne and I had spent most of our lives by the east coast we decided to camp in Wales. We met up at a crossroads near Corwen and she trailed us westwards along the A5. It was August and the roads were busy. The campsites we passed were either full or too near the main road. Once past Porthmadog we knew we would have to find somewhere soon if we were to erect two tents before nightfall. In a remote spot in the middle of the Llŷn peninsula we stopped by a farm to ask where the nearest campsite was. The sight of three tired adults, four fractious children and a dog desperate to jump out of our car, or maybe the prospect of adding to his income by embarking on unexpected diversification, spurred the farmer into offering us a field, and the use of his toilet.

Having pitched camp, helped by the light of a full moon, we crawled into our makeshift sleeping bags and decided that we would look no further for an official campsite. We had privacy, a fine view, a friendly farmer and a toilet. Who could ask for more? The weather was fine; the sea was all around us and the beaches were superb. The investiture of the Prince of Wales had taken place that year, so we visited Caernarfon castle. On the last day there was to be a special treat. We could not come to North Wales without a trip on the Ffestiniog railway.

Leaving our cars at Pwllheli we travelled by Diesel to Minffordd and crossed over to the Ffestiniog line. In steamed a long and crowded train. By the time we had stowed away the pushchair and sorted out four small children and our Labrador, Sheba, the only hope of a seat was in a cattle wagon, which already looked solid with passengers. We spent the upward journey like the central occupants of a sardine tin. We tried to enthral Daphne with descriptions of the wonderful views she would have been able to see if: a) there was a proper window; b) she didn't have five portly male rail enthusiasts fighting for the only existing openings in which to poke their cameras, and c) if she didn't have two children and a dog's head resting on her lap.

I contented myself by gazing through a hole in the floor at the sleepers and ballast on the track beneath, while Michael sat against a basket bulging with flasks, nappies and potties, gazing in frustration at his redundant ciné camera. The children, for whom this was to be THE BIG TREAT, had nodded off to sleep, mesmerised by the rhythmic clickety-clack of the train on the track.

Most people disembarked at Tan-y-Bwlch, but we stayed on to marvel at the re-opened section up to Dduallt. Here we disgorged our little families and climbed onto a grassy mound, where I showed off my newly acquired knowledge of how to pronounce this station's name, which looked so daunting to our English eyes and tongues.

'Try saying "Theeacht" as if you were bringing up phlegm', advised a shopkeeper in Pwllheli.

My throat was already sore with trying to get the 'll' sound correct in Pwllheli, but he would not rest until I had mastered Dduallt.

Before I would unload the picnic basket I had to ensure that Michael and Daphne had emulated my Welsh pronunciation skill. We then ate, played hide-and-seek, and watched another train come in. Sheba, who was crossed with a Collie, was rather too keen to round up the mountain sheep, so we decided to take this train down and have a walk around the lake near Tan-y-Bwlch. We had only just managed to get our contingent and paraphernalia onto the train when it seemed time to disembark at Tan-y-Bwlch platform.

Daphne was having trouble reassembling the pushchair and discovered that a wing nut was missing. Michael and I leapt back onto the train, crawled between people's legs, looked under seats and enlisted the help of the guard.

'Take your time,' he said. 'I should get all your party back on the train, if I were you. There's so many people up at Dduallt that anyone hoping to get the next train down won't stand a cat in hell's chance of getting on.'

So Daphne collapsed the failing pushchair once more and rounded up the children to get on the train again.

'Pauline, Pauline?' Where was Pauline?

No sign of our two-year-old, so we jumped off the train and began a frantic search. Daphne combed the station, Michael ran off up the track, and I ran down the road towards the lake. Five minutes later, and still no Pauline. Had she got back on the train and was even now hurtling down on her parentless way to Porthmadog? Daphne ran to ask the stationmaster to ring up Porthmadog station to say that there might be a lone two-year old girl on the train. If so, would they please keep her safe until we could collect her?

I felt ashamed and completely inept as a mother. Daphne had coped admirably with her two children and a lopsided pushchair. I had the support of a husband, but between us we hadn't managed to look after our two children and a dog.

Dog? Dog? Where was the dog?

We had no memory of putting her onto the train at Dduallt. Maybe she had given chase to the sheep and had therefore been shot by a distraught farmer. Or maybe she had tried to follow our train down the track and had been mown down by the up train. With only a sliver of hope in my heart I ran to the stationmaster to enlist his help again.

'I know you've just rung down to Porthmadog to tell them to look after our two-year-old daughter, but could you just ring up to Dduallt and ask them to look after a lone Labrador, who might just be sitting on the platform?'

While the stationmaster was deciding whether to report me to the NSPCC or the RSPCA, Michael appeared, beaming, with Pauline clutching his hand. She had had a dramatic rescue from the track just in front of the up train.

'I look for trains' she said. 'Nice driver man picked me up.'

I soon shattered my husband's short-lived smugness by dropping the bombshell about the dog. He thrust Pauline into my waiting arms and ran off across the rough moorland in a bid to find Sheba.

Daphne said, unconvincingly, 'It's a lovely railway,' and proceeded to buy me a cup of tea to soothe my shattered nerves.

A party of American tourists asked me if I knew the time of the next train.

'Well,' I began, 'the train down will probably be late because when it was on its way up the driver had to stop to retrieve my daughter. And it may be even later leaving Dduallt to come down because the station staff there are looking for my dog.'

The Americans obviously thought that I had 'lost it' completely and went off down the platform to consult a large clock on a sandwich board which advertised the up and down train times. They were not amused to see two children twiddling the hands round as fast as they could go. Neither was I. They were my children.

Hopefully I set both sides to read 4.30 p.m. But hark! What was this coming down the line? It was the down train and, joy of joys, there was Michael complete with Sheba, who had been found waiting patiently on Dduallt station with the lead in her mouth. The excitement of seeing daddy and dog was too much for Pauline who fell backwards off the station seat and let out an ear-piercing scream. I picked up the remains and made for the carriage door.

'Not so fast,' said the guard. There's no room on this train.'

I didn't have time to tell him of our awful adventures, that we had to get to Minffordd or we would miss our connection, that we had four children under five who were desperate for a meal, and that we still hadn't found the wing nut from the pushchair. Instead I turned on the tears, which were already welling up in my eyes, and somehow he managed to push us all into the last compartment.

Cooking our fish fingers by torchlight outside the tent that night we were glad that this was the last day of our holidays, and that a return to normality was nigh. Daphne certainly had no intention of going away with the vicar again.

I knew I had to!

Chapter Nine

Gypsy Rose Lea had once told me at Hull Fair that I would 'go west'. This was pretty well guaranteed for anyone living in Hull. However, to disprove this, Michael pursued the offer of the living of Easington, near Spurn Point. He had served two curacies in contrasting parishes and was now looking for an incumbency. We visited the parish, talked with the churchwardens, measured up the vicarage for carpets and typed the letter of acceptance to the Lord Chancellor, who was patron of this living.

We could have posted the letter on the Friday, but Michael felt intuitively that he should wait until the post had arrived on the Saturday morning. He was right to have waited, for in the post was a letter from the trustees of the vacant living of St. Jude's in Halifax, inviting him for an interview. Whereas Michael viewed this as divine intervention, I was not pleased with God for this redirection. I was already looking forward to living by the sea, and had even bought a new red stair carpet to fit Easington vicarage. I knew that I was going to have to say, 'nevertheless, not my will but thine be done', and leave the issue in God's hands.

On the day that we were due to drive over to Halifax to survey the scene, our car would not start. (Was this another case of God's intervention, I wondered?) It was not. Michael's father volunteered to drive us in his car. As we approached the parish he experienced a sense of déjà vu. This was the parish he had been asked to consider some twelve years earlier, but he had not pursued this on account of Michael's pending 'A' level exams.

During those past twelve years Michael had gone on to university in Lampeter, to theological college in Birkenhead, married me, served curacies in York and Hull and become father to two children. He was soon to be chosen as the new incumbent of the parish of St. Jude, with its imposing millstone grit church, built with money from Victorian magnates in Halifax: Crossley of carpet fame, and Baldwin, who with Paton was 'big' in wool, and whose representatives still served as patrons of the living. The imposing vicarage, facing 70 acres of parkland, was built in 1895 and had five reception rooms, five large bedrooms, five attic bedrooms, three cellars and two staircases. The new red stair carpet chosen for Easington vicarage just fitted one of the staircases, and joined on admirably to the red carpet which had once graced the Hull study, and which now filled the spacious landing.

Gypsy Rose Lea had been right – we had gone west. It was under God's guidance rather than hers, and looking back I am so thankful that we don't always go where we think is best at the time. It was in Halifax that all our children started their schooling and, as we stayed for 14 years, Christopher both started and finished his schooling there. St. Jude's with its fine musical tradition and vibrant, growing congregation held out many opportunities and challenges. We had faced the physical demands of packing up one home and repacking into another. Michael hadn't bargained on the mental and spiritual demands incurred in moving from being a curate to becoming a vicar. I certainly hadn't predicted that the emergence from my curate's wife chrysalis into a full-blown vicar's wife would be so swift and life changing.

'Will you come to the magazine meeting on Wednesday, Mrs Walker? I'm sure your 'resident' will baby-sit for you.'

Did they really think that a 29-year-old whose family had survived on £500 p.a. for the past six years would be able to afford a daily, let alone a resident maid?

'Would you consider becoming Enrolling Member of the Mothers' Union? We like our vicar's wife to be at the helm.'

'Do you sing in the choir?'

'The June magazine is due out on the last Sunday of May – I've heard you can type.'

'You couldn't test three Guides for their cook's badge could you?'

Before the onset of a busy parish programme starting up again in September we knew we needed a holiday. Christopher would be five in July and Pauline almost two and a half. They hadn't seen their auntie and uncle and four cousins in south-west England for a very long time, so we jumped at the chance of a fortnight near them. We scanned the Church Times adverts, and out jumped:

'Holiday exchange. We would like to exchange our large vicarage in south-west England for two weeks with large one in scenic part of north of England. Would welcome children and well-behaved dog. Duties to include Sunday services at three village churches and feeding of cats.'

We applied straight away, hoping that the mention of 'Halifax' would not be off-putting. People still had an image of our town being the capital of dark satanic mill-land. Photos of the view from our house, with brochures of accessible dales and moors, did the trick. The exchange vicar and family were happy to come.

Convinced that Mrs Exchange-Vicar would have a certificate in health and hygiene, I armed myself with scrubbing brush and spray polish, stacked towels neatly in the airing cupboard, removed spilt flour and sugar from my shelves and cleaned and labelled every drawer with adhesive labels, proclaiming the rightful home for tea towels, rotary whisks and Brillo pads. After five days of being a full time Mrs Mop I was certainly ready for a holiday. So was Michael who had tidied his study to an unbelievable degree and left neat lists of service times, lay readers, and undertakers.

We were hot and weary on our journey from Yorkshire to the south-west. These were pre-motorway days, so it took many hours. As we approached the picturesque village we felt a surge of energy and excitement. The vicarage was lovely – large and L-shaped with an east wing. At least it had when we arrived. Orlando miaowed a welcome and a note in the hallway wished us a happy stay and invited us to pick any flowers, beans, beet, potatoes or fruit from their prolific garden. Immediately I felt a sense of guilt. Our Pennine garden was not in the same league. I sincerely hoped that our exchange family was happy with scraggy heather.

My guilty feelings were assuaged when I walked into the kitchen. An ancient Aga belched fumes, the table was full of crumbs, unwashed cups and dirty tea towels on which slept Orlando's brother and sister. Michael went on a tour of the bedrooms and reported a three-inch dust layer under all the beds. The children traced a repulsive smell to the algae-congealed bowl where, beyond a green curtain of slime, two unfortunate goldfish were struggling for survival. Housekeeping was certainly not the degree subject of my counterpart. I thought smugly of my pristine cutlery drawer and sparkling windows in Halifax, then came down to earth with a bump as I realised that before I could enjoy my fortnight's holiday I would have to spend the first two days in a major spring clean.

Further exploration had revealed an odd room – probably once a butler's pantry – in which was housed a bewildering selection of electrical apparatus, with radios, ear-phones, aerials and instructions of where the villagers were to bunk in the event of a nuclear attack. After seeing this I vowed never again to complain about Michael's obsession with railways. There were far more eccentric hobbies among his fellow clergy!

We decided to let the belching Aga go out. It was a hot August and we would be out on the beach or with my sister and family most days, and I could easily manage to cook on our two camping gas stoves. I cleaned up an area of kitchen table as my cooking area while Michael and the children went into the immaculate garden to pick raspberries for tea. Suddenly Christopher ran in.

'Daddy's got a bee up his bottom!' he shouted.

I ordered Michael to whip off his shorts and underpants and to lie down on the kitchen floor so that I could straddle him and pluck out the offending sting.

'Hello – it's Monica here – just coming in to welcome you to our parish and tell you...'

We never knew what Monica was going to tell us. She peered round the door and took one look at the semi-naked exchange vicar with a woman straddled across his prone body and decided to leave, never to return.

There were more communicants than we had expected at the village church the next morning. Curiosity had ensured a good turnout.

Maybe it was curiosity that had killed the cat too. On arrival we had read the instructions: 'Please give Kitekat to Sandy, Marmalade, and Orlando and Felix.' The first three cats who used the pantry shelves or kitchen table for bedrooms were soon accounted for, but where was Felix? We organised search parties around the vicarage and garden, investigated potting sheds and garage, but all to no avail. The next two evenings we walked round the village lanes calling, 'Felix! Felix!' Still no fourth cat.

There was a lingering putrid smell in the vicarage dining room. It was not the goldfish bowl – I had dealt with that. Michael's theory was dead rats under the floorboard. I wondered if it was the corpse of the elusive Felix. I picked the short straw and had to ring back to our Halifax vicarage to confess the loss of Felix and ask for an audio identikit picture of the missing moggie.

'Felix!' shrieked the vicar's wife.

'We haven't got a Felix.'

'But the note said we were to give Kitekat to Sandy, Marmalade, Orlando and Felix.'

'No, the Felix is in addition to the Kitekat – it's on the top pantry shelf,' she answered, in an exasperated tone.

I was going to have to break the news to our family that we had wasted two evening shouting up and down country lanes for cat food.

Meanwhile I was chatting down the phone thanking 'Mrs I-don't-hoover-under-beds' for the lovely fruit and vegetables on which we were living. I asked how they were enjoying Yorkshire, but her reply was lost amid a high-pitched yapping. Could one small dog produce that volume of sound?

No. One small dog could not. But five small dogs could. We had taken our well-behaved Labrador with us on the understanding that they would bring one well-behaved terrier to Halifax. On our return our parishioners assured us that there had been five wild ones. We soon saw, with dismay, where these unfortunates had been imprisoned by day – in our master bedroom. The windows were permanently etched by the claws of those frantic dogs.

If our Halifax parishioners had been on the verge of calling out the RSPCA then the parishioners in the village where we were staying only just escaped calling out the fire brigade. On our last day we attempted to relight the Aga. Michael went out to gather fuel, while I finished off packing and hoovered under the beds. Michael returned to the kitchen in the nick of time. The Aga fire was roaring. I had left the camping gas stove on top. Next to it was a rapidly expanding spare gas canister. As Michael walked in he saw its distorted body roll off. A minute later it could have exploded and saved the diocesan parsonage officer the difficult decision of whether or not to demolish the East wing. Not that a big bang would have worried the villagers unduly. They had been well prepared by their eccentric vicar on what actions to take in the event of an explosion.

We escaped from our holiday home leaving the parishioners with the excitement of telling their vicar about the strange family from Yorkshire who went around yelling 'Felix', not to mention the vicar and wife who had been found in a compromising position on the kitchen floor.

I hope the goldfish survived. I hope the smell was not dead rats under the floorboards. And I hope the vicar will never have to put his early-warning system into action.

Be warned, all ye who dream of idyllic vicarage exchanges. Verily, verily I say unto you, such Church Times adverts are a snare and delusion. Camping's really much safer!

Chapter Ten

Was camping safer? Camping was certainly changing fast and our simple three-berth, orange tent was soon to look antique amid a flurry of modern tents with extensions, canopies and verandas. Some smaller ones even had poles that sprang into place automatically when released from their constraining bag, and by now you could buy self-inflating igloos. Camping shops were opening up selling all the must-have add-ons which any self-respecting camper should acquire: stoves with four burners and even an oven, hanging lights, pantry shelves, cool boxes, dining table and chairs, luxurious camp beds and sleeping bags to cocoon yourself in the current seasonal tog value. None of these items was in our price range and we took a perverted pride in being 'proper campers'.

Even now, in our vintage years, we sleep on the ground, albeit on blow-up airbeds and in our 1980s sleeping bags, and we still rely on a torch for light, and cook ingenious recipes on two camping gas stoves. We have bought two chairs from where we can sit and savour the scenes around us as new campers arrive and sort out their canvas villages, hook up to the electricity supply so that they can plug in their fridge, fan, heater, cooker, television and computer. Many surround their enclaves with canvas windbreaks, and corral themselves into little suburbs of Liverpool or Birmingham. But we are grateful. Without them our hobby of people-viewing would be the poorer.

All this is a far cry from my first camping experiences with the Girl Guides in the early 1950s. Our luggage consisted of a sailor's type kitbag with a drawstring top, and a homemade sleeping bag made from a sewn-up sheet inside a rough, grey wartime blanket fastened together with safety pins. We did not have pillows. Our heads rested on our kitbags stuffed with our clean (and dirty) underwear. We wore Guide uniform every day, but were allowed shorts instead of skirts, should the weather turn warmer – which it never did.

I was twelve when I went on my first camp; it was to Sawley, near Ripon, and it was my first time away from home. I loved it and couldn't wait to go again. The following year I was a patrol leader and was in charge of my tent and its six occupants. My tie was pressed, lanyard whitened, belt polished and penknife hooked on, complete with attachments for opening tins and extracting stones from horses' hooves. (Did anyone ever find a hobbling horse in need of such treatment?) Thirty Guides were lifted up and posted into the side of a local removal firm's largest van. We had no window, little ventilation, and certainly no safety belts. We sat on top of our kitbags and in semi-darkness were swayed and sometimes tossed on our fifty mile journey to Appletreewick in Wharfedale. The previous week this van had been carefully loaded with people's precious furniture, strapped in with webbing and carefully padded with blankets to save any damage. We girls, on the other hand, had to cling on to each other as we rounded corners and were sometimes buried under avalanches of dixies and billycans.

I don't remember our parents having to sign complicated forms entrusting their little darlings' lives to the Guide captain, helpers or van driver. We were certainly not given any faddy food options or expected to have allergies. Our wartime generation was brought up to eat everything and be thankful, notwithstanding grey bread, oily margarine, rabbit pies, too many carrots, and far too much cabbage. Camp fare was substantial and almost palatable if you were hungry after an afternoon's hike, closed your eyes and thought of England.

Each patrol took its turn in the daily camp duties. The cooks cooked and then had the most horrid job of all – cleaning the soot-blackened pans. The orderlies had the pleasanter job of setting out the plates and cutlery in a circle on the grass (Guide camps had not by then graduated to marquees). They had to ensure that the site was tidy and all plates washed and drained on wooden racks, which the wood patrol had made using complicated square-lashing techniques. Being in the wood or the messenger patrol was a 'doddle'. The former went for long walks and returned with kindling wood, larger sticks and logs for the campfire. The latter went to the village shop for bread and meat, and posted cards declaring to our parents that everyone was having a wonderful time – not mentioning that two of the girls had been so homesick that they had cried all night and had to be moved to Captain's tent.

The most horrid daily task was allocated to the Health patrol. On arrival they had to dig out trenches in the farthest part of the farmer's field and erect somewhat flimsy sack-like material on frames to give a modicum of privacy to those who really had to 'go' to the latrines. Each compartment was furnished with a shovel and a mound of earth with which to bury the contents of our daily offerings. Nose masks would have been a welcome addition.

Our living quarters were bell tents, with a central pole, and we slept, unconventionally, with our heads by the pole, radiating outwards, so that they were the furthest away from inquisitive spiders, mice or earwigs. Up the pole was lashed a sturdy tree branch, from whose twigs hung our 'health bags' and outside, to hold our wellies, was a somewhat shaky shoe rack, another product of our square-lashing lessons. Captain and Lieutenant examined each tent every morning and awarded points for the tidiest. After breakfast we stood in a circle around the flagpole and solemnly raised our colours, saluted and sang the national anthem. In the evening we lowered the colours with equal solemnity. As we sang 'God save the Queen' we thought excitedly of her coronation the following week. The weather had already started to deteriorate in preparation for a very wet June 2nd for this national celebration.

Nonetheless we sat outside in a circle on our waterproof mats, round the campfire, singing 'Ging Gang Gooli Gooli Gooli Gooli Watcha, Ging Gang Goo'; 'Land of the silver birch, home of the beaver'; and one called 'Donkey-riding' which started 'Were you ever in Quebec, stowing timber on the deck?' No I never had that privilege, but I did enjoy taking off my belt and clanking the metal clasps together to imitate the clip clop of the donkey. We sang of 'Little Johnny England' who went a-wandering, of 'Johnny Appleseed', and then 'Campfire's burning' sung to a round, before ending with 'Day is done...' the traditional Guiding evening hymn, bizarrely known as TAPS.

Warmed with an enamel mug of cocoa we went back to our tents, to sing a bit more, to wiggle our hips into a more comfortable position on the ground, to prod our unyielding kitbag pillows, to talk and giggle, and perchance to sleep.

My patrol had not been happy about my decision to pitch our tent at the top of the grassy slope. All other patrols had their tents at the bottom, by a swiftly flowing stream. I had to admit that I had some sympathy with my girls as they grumbled about climbing up the steep slope after every activity. However my decision to stay put was vindicated early in the week. About an hour after we had snuggled into our sleeping bags we heard an ominous thunder roll. I was terrified of lightning, but couldn't exhibit any fear in front of the younger girls. I put on my boots, went out to adjust the guy ropes, and told them all to make sure their belongings were well away from the walls of the tent. They had already had dire warnings not to touch the canvas. Old-fashioned tents let water in if you so much as brushed past their insides.

Then we heard noise and saw torchlights flashing below. The beck had burst its banks and invaded neighbouring tents. The evacuation onto the top of the slope took two hours. My patrol helped, and we all had to stifle the desire to say, 'I told you so'. There were only two casualties. One was the lemonade and milk supply. We had suspended nets containing our bottles from a branch above the stream, in an effort to keep them cool in the water. Next morning they were nowhere to be seen. Neither was the post box, which had also been hanging on a branch. However Captain found it further downstream, and retrieved the sodden postcards. My friend Pamela added a PS on the card to her grandma, 'Sorry – very wet; fell in stream.' Two days later (yes, the post was fast and reliable then) Pamela received a large parcel from her grandma in Lincolnshire, with a note saying, 'Sorry to hear you had fallen in the stream – here are some warm jumpers and a skirt.'

On the last night of our camp we had a fancy dress competition. The winning patrol fully deserved their prize of a big bar of chocolate; they had dressed up as mountaineers, and roped themselves together, putting on a credible performance of hacking their way up the slope and then planting the Union Jack and posing for a photo. They were 'The Everest Expedition'. News of the actual conquest of Everest was apparently delayed so that it could be broadcast on the following Tuesday, Coronation Day. I like to think that as our Guides planted their flag, so Hillary and Tensing were planting theirs. We, and they, were on top of the world. A new era was dawning – the age of Elizabeth – 'God save the Queen'.

Chapter Eleven

Elizabeth had been Queen for twenty years when our third baby arrived. It was a girl, but this time I managed to produce a smaller one – only nine pounds six ounces! She was christened Rosemary Elizabeth, in St Jude's Church, Halifax.

For over eighty years the font had been just inside the main door into church, in a poky corner with electric light switches and hymnbooks. This was where the newest members of the church were welcomed. But what a welcome! It was like opening the door to a visitor and then keeping them standing on the doorstep rather than inviting them into the main room. The decision to move the font into a central position beneath the west window was democratically taken at a Parochial Church Council meeting, and of course was subject to the archdeacon's approval and that of the diocese, after faculty forms had been filled in and approved. To judge by the fallout you would have thought that the poor vicar had moved the font himself in the middle of the night without any consultation.

'Our Bert was christened in that font in the corner; if it was good enough for him to be done there it's good enough for anybody.'

I sensed a swelling of undercurrent opposition from some of the more vociferous members of the congregation. I could foresee a stormy ride at the next Council meeting.

I was not on the Parochial Church Council. I have never been on any PCC and never intend being on one. When I became engaged to Michael his mother had given me two pieces of advice: one was to learn to make a good pineapple pudding (his favourite) and the other was not to be inveigled onto the PCC. She had weakened and been on one for a year or two, but found it didn't work for her. Much of the business she already knew about anyway, and she was helping the church by putting her skills to use through her writing, her speaking, her visiting, her position in the Mothers' Union and her aptitude for arranging social events and vicarage tea-parties. At the PCC meetings she found it hard to take an opposite view to that of her husband. Conversely, when she did agree with him – most of the time – she resented vehement opposition from others, especially that laced with vitriol. When they openly criticised her husband she confessed to me that she had wanted to scratch their eyes out. Such feelings did neither her nor anyone else any good, so she declined the invitation to stand for election at the following Easter's AGM.

Following her advice I continued to decline any such invitations. Some clergy wives did serve on their church councils, and to good effect. Maybe I was a coward, but I sensed that I was serving Michael better by being impartial. I was a sounding board from which he could bounce off all the outpourings from the meetings. Occasionally I could wholeheartedly agree with those who had put up opposing views to his. Had I been at the meeting my wifely allegiance would have clouded my true judgement. Mostly, though, I could sympathise with his feelings of frustration or despair when everyone had seemed against him, and I would listen to a re-enactment of the meeting as he tossed and turned and eventually dozed off into a fitful sleep. He had 'got it off his chest' and part of it had landed on mine. That was what marriage was all about: 'All that I have I share with you... including nightmares of the entire congregation surrounding the vicarage intoning to a suitable psalm chant, 'Away with the vicar / for he has / moved the font: it should have stayed in the corner, where it has / been / since the / church was built.'

Rosemary Elizabeth was the third baby to be baptised in the newly sited font. Unlike the first two, she was baptised in a main service of the day. Grandpa Walker had to travel to Halifax after taking two morning services in Beverley, so the baptism took place during evensong. As I walked into the church, bearing our five-week-old daughter, resplendent in family heirloom Victorian christening gown, I spied in the back pew the main opponents of the wretched 'font move'. As evensong progressed I had visions of them behind us, muttering and grumbling and poised for post-service attack.

When we reached the time for the baptism, suddenly they had no cover. We all turned to face the font, which was proudly standing centre stage back. The revolutionaries were now in prime viewing position. Grandpa was unusually nervous at taking a baptism in front of the entire family, and Rosemary did not help by lashing out her little arm as he lifted up the shell containing the baptismal water. She showered him and his prayer book, then looked up with her cornflower blue eyes into his, and he smiled back. So did the anti-font brigade. That water not only quenched the fiery darts of the devil, but it also quenched the fiery darts of the back pew dwellers. After the service the hitherto militant ringleader shook hands warmly with Michael, and made my cup of happiness complete when I heard her say, 'Font looks right good there, after all. Take back all I've said. No hard feelings. Shows up carving on front of font; never saw that there boat when it was in shadows in corner. Any case we had a right good view from back pew. Lovely service.'

That was the best West Riding apology one could have hoped for. I would send her a bit of christening cake!

Soon after Rosemary's baptism a teacher asked if we would have a 12-year-old French girl to stay for three weeks. Her classmates were coming to Halifax on a pupil exchange, but this girl was an orphan and could not offer return hospitality. That was fine by us; our children were seven, five and two months, and not yet into the realms of learning French. The following July we had a surprise telephone call from another French girl announcing that she was coming to look after our children and would be arriving on Saturday at 'Lids'. Wires had been crossed. Our orphan was unable to come, and the French exchange authorities had it in their heads that we wanted an au pair. It was too late to alter arrangements. We would accept whoever came. We pored over the road atlas to find anything just across the Channel resembling Lids, and decided that the flight must be from Brittany to Lydd in Kent.

When we phoned France to give complicated directions from Kent to West Yorkshire the girl insisted we had got it wrong. It would take only just over fifty minutes. Only then did we twig that she was flying to Leeds. Michael arranged to meet the au pair that we didn't really need. He took one look at tall, elegant and shapely 18-year-old Nadine and quickly changed his views. We definitely did need an au pair!

She stayed with us for three weeks, was wonderful with the children, and we were able to help her expand her already extensive English vocabulary.

It wasn't just words that she learned, but some useful idioms and expressions. On her first evening Michael took Nadine over to view the church. Ronnie, the verger, was preparing for the Sunday services, so Michael introduced Nadine to him. Back at the vicarage Nadine confided in me, 'I do not like zat man'.

'Why?' I asked. 'What did he say?'

'When Michael introduced me he shook my hand, and said, "Oh, I'll look forward to seeing more of you."

I am not going to show him any more of me' said Nadine, hastily pulling her cardigan round her bare shoulders.

★ ★ ★

Before going to bed Nadine told us that her mother had said she must warn us that her daughter talked in her sleep and sometimes screamed loudly. We were not to be frightened. We assured her that this was a vicarage – a holy house – and that she was most unlikely to scream during her stay. Our psychology worked. Silence reigned at night. Well, it did until we took her camping.

Nadine was keen to see another part of Britain, so we took her to the Lake District. Our ancient tent, a three-berth one, had been fine for Michael, Christopher, baby Pauline and me. Now we had to add Rosemary, a large Golden Labrador, and a tall, albeit slender, French girl. The dog was relegated to the grass outside the inner tent. For propriety's sake Michael slept by the door, then all of our family in age order, and finally, at the far end, Nadine. Unfortunately we had pitched on a slope. When Michael rolled over in his sleep it was a case of 'and they all rolled over and one dropped off...' Nadine, with the weight of the Walker family on top of her, was driven into nightmare mode and let out a blood-chilling scream followed by a hysterical, 'Oh Maman, oh Maman!' which awoke the entire campsite who shone their torches at us, watching incredulously as three adults, three children and a dog disgorged from such a small tent.

Nadine added her name to the list of unfortunates who had clocked up unforgettable experiences when away with the vicar. The list was about to grow...

Chapter Twelve

We were on the verge of buying a bigger tent when Michael's colleague and wife asked if we would contemplate crewing for them on a narrowboat holiday. We could hire an eight-berth boat and enjoy a peaceful cruise along the Coventry and Grand Union canals. They had no children at that time, but assured us that our children, who were now nine, six and eighteen months, would be quite safe and would all love the experience.

As there was a spare berth we invited a friend to join us. She was a little apprehensive about sharing such cramped quarters, but agreed to come if we promised not to sit our youngest on her potty in the living area. Given the minimal specifications of a canal boat toilet room I could foresee difficulties in granting this request. In the event I didn't have to worry, as the friend contracted a stomach bug just before the holiday was due to start and had to cancel. However she insisted on supplying all the items that she had promised to bring for our communal use.

Our boat, 'Altostratus', was awaiting us at Hillmorton, near Rugby. Rain was lashing down, so I was bundled onto the boat with the children and the dog while the others donned waterproofs and started to unload the two cars. In between receiving soggy cartons of groceries, putting them in cupboards and entertaining three children I tried to make some tea. The older children were squabbling about who should have the top bunk, the dog was blocking the passage way, Rosemary was sitting in earnest concentration on her potty and I was skidding about on the wet floor looking for the bread. The other three adults were cold, wet and irritable. Blood sugars were running low, so I decided on honey sandwiches, having found in our absent friend's cardboard box a large jar bearing the label 'Yorkshire Wild Honey'. It was rather a violent shade of yellow and certainly had an unusual consistency as I spread it lavishly on slices of a whole loaf. I had dropped some honey on the cooker, so scooped it up onto my middle finger and licked it.

At this point may I remind you to avoid decanting any alien substances into jars unless you have removed the existing label and very clearly relabelled the jar with its new contents. I had spent the last twenty minutes and a whole large loaf in the manufacture of a new variety of sandwiches that were certainly not to be recommended for vicarage tea parties. Mental note – stick to cucumber, and do not serve Swarfega sandwiches. I gagged, spat, rinsed and gagged again. In later bouts of sickness when yesterday's takeaway was making a return journey up my oesophagus I took comfort in the fact that the taste was far less revolting than regurgitated Swarfega.

We hadn't enough bread on board to make more sandwiches, so I brewed up tea.

'We can't drink tea now – we've got to move from the moorings and get under way.'

I put the mugs of tea on the table until a more suitable moment arrived. It did not. The boat struck the side of the canal under a bridge and shook so violently that the mugs slid off, and the tea joined the pools of water on the cabin floor. I was longing to go up on deck and see the scenery, but the others were leaping around with poles and ropes, and the rain was now blowing horizontally.

'We could do with some tea now!' they shouted down.

'I could do with getting the next train back to Halifax,' I thought.

The children were fractious and the adults not much better. I was between the devil and the deep muddy canal water. The Swarfega had not helped to sweeten my taste buds or my mood. I had had enough.

As I lay on my bunk the next morning, planning my imminent return train trip with the children back to Halifax, I drew back the curtains and saw wild flowers waving in the breeze, rabbits playing in the fields and a flotilla of ducklings paddling along in the rippling sun-dappled water. Church bells were ringing. Suddenly God was in his heaven and all was right with the world. Maybe Robert Browning had been inspired on such a morning. I would have to delay my return trip for another day.

By the end of that day I had fallen victim to canal addiction. Christopher and Pauline, looking like mini-

Michelin men in their fat orange life jackets, ran up and down the towpath and helped work the locks, while Rosemary was strapped into her pushchair lashed to the bows with my best Girl Guide knots. From her magnificent vantage point she could wave to oncoming boats and observe the flowers, the nests and the bird life. It was an ideal preparation for a child destined to study botany and biology. Sheba, our dog, was having a wonderful taste of canal towpath freedom, with the added excitement of rabbits, and Michael was realising how often canal and rail routes converged. This was approaching heaven. I cooked an impressive Sunday lunch complete with lemon meringue pie, and quietly hid the train timetable. I had decided to stay.

For the next few years our holidays included canals. Not the leisurely holidays mentioned in the brochures. Oh no! Not for us the late morning starts, the lunchtime mooring for a siesta, the canal-side afternoon tea or the gargantuan meal in the evening at the pub. We cast off at dawn and ate in relays, not turning off the engine until dusk approached. The two-week circuit recommended in the brochure was to be done by the Walker family in one week. We wore out a succession of one-time friends locking up and down the Hatton, Tardebigge and Foxton flights of locks.

The year we did the Cheshire Ring route we had to sing a funeral dirge as we left Manchester, having had a morning fruitlessly searching for our Labrador dog, last seen on the towpath in the city centre. We had to keep on the move to be sure of getting our hire boat back to the depot by Friday evening. The children cried, Michael promised to hitch a lift back into Manchester once we had moored, and to contact the police, and I tried to put on a brave face as I prepared a belated lunch. Tears started dropping into the stew; sobs were starting to well up so I made a dash to the only private place on board – the loo. The door wouldn't budge. Maybe the towels had dropped off their hook behind the door. I pushed harder and the obstruction moved. Sheba had been stuck there all morning. Suddenly it was Resurrection Day and we chugged on with an Easter song in our hearts.

We sang the delights of canal holidays to Malcolm, who had been a fellow curate with Michael in Hull, and his wife Janet. They were brave enough to accept our invitation to join them on a circuit starting from Birmingham. Any visions they had had about cruising through flower-strewn meadows were quickly shattered as we snaked between Victorian warehouses and factories. From the lofty window of one of these appeared a head, followed by an arm throwing out to us a huge ball of plastic rope. Michael caught it. The head disappeared from view; we chugged on. We could only assume that the man had stolen it and at the approach of his boss had thrown out the incriminating evidence. We stuck it under the table – we had no time to deliberate on its future – there were locks to be done. On the lock beam were bundles of papers. Knowing how useful papers were to put down on the cabin floor in the event of rain, Michael threw the bundle down to me on the boat. Later, on closer examination, we realised it was subversive IRA literature.

'Better not have the police on board,' said Malcolm, 'what with stolen rope and IRA literature.'

As we approached a greener area in the suburbs we realised that our lights would not work. Mobile phones had not yet been invented. Michael and Malcolm tied up the boat and ran off down the towpath to find a phone to ring the boat-hirer to ask for advice. Janet and I read a bedtime story to the children, then Janet remarked, 'Look at those lovely flowers.' By the time I had stood up to peer out of the window, the flowers had disappeared. Truth dawned. We were adrift. Our husbands needed to go on a crash course in knotting. We poled our way to the bank and moored afresh. By the time the men had returned and mended the lights we didn't really need electricity, as it was time for bed. We had just nodded off when we were awakened by loud and lewd singing. It was the Saturday night 'boozy boat' passing with its well-oiled passengers aboard.

Christopher, who had qualified as a helmsman on a junior navigation course, was on the tiller as we set off at dawn; the rest of us were having breakfast, which was interrupted by his insistent shouts that he had seen a body in the canal. Michael put the boat in reverse. Christopher was right. It was a matter for the police. Michael knocked at the door of the cottage at the canal junction. He can't remember what he said, but he can still remember the flimsy blue negligee of the lock-keeper's daughter. She alerted the emergency services, and before we could hide the stolen rope and the IRA literature we had both the fire brigade and the police on board. The children insisted on watching the proceedings.

'It's my body – I found it first!' claimed Christopher, who was most upset at not being asked to go to the police station to give evidence. Michael had to do this, and returned to tell us that the body had been that of a very old lady who had not had long to live anyway. Nonetheless it was sad to think of her end coming in this way, whether by design or accident.

It was a sobering start to our holiday, but we tried not to let it spoil our week. I don't think Malcolm and Janet were going to become canal converts. Malcolm revealed at the end of our cruise that he didn't really enjoy being on water as he didn't swim. We had tried to give them cheer in the form of a bottle of bubbly to celebrate their wedding anniversary, but because we were behind time in our schedule as a result of the 'incident' we had to use this bottle on our final stretch of canal to bribe the lock-keeper to let us through before he clocked off duty.

At the boat depot we binned the literature, but kept the rope. We were to need it for later holidays on the water. Meanwhile Michael had decided to give canal holidays a break and to try something different. I was filled with curiosity and apprehension when he announced that before next summer we would have to acquire some equestrian knowledge, and a modicum of Welsh.

Chapter Thirteen

Your horse is called Woolly, and he's Welsh. He knows the route like the back of his hoof, and you'll find that he stops at every pub on the route and won't walk on until you've bought him a bag of crisps.' This was our introduction to the large beast who was to pull our Romany caravan around the Talgarth and Crickhowell areas of Wales. I gazed up at him in awe and in fright.

Horses were not really my scene. The nearest I had been to them was on the racecourse at Beverley, where I was born and brought up. Father had taken me to Beverley races and shown me the rudiments of gambling – though never more than 'a shilling each way'. When I was twelve my mother had to go to Birmingham to look after my grandpa; I was left in charge of the cooking and the housekeeping money. Thursday was Race Day; father had gone off after lunch with his binoculars, but I had to go back to school. At four o'clock I cycled up to the racecourse, left my bike in the care of a friendly young policeman and paid a shilling to get onto the course. Just in time for the 4.30 p.m. race I used another shilling from the housekeeping purse to back the favourite, who duly won. Flushed with success I put two shillings on 'Crusader's Horn' in the last race, and was thrilled at its success and at my substantial winnings.

I freewheeled down the hill and managed to be home with the table laid before father's return.

'Did you have a good afternoon, Dad?' I asked solicitously.

'Well, I was doing all right until the last race, and then I put all my winnings on the favourite and it was beaten.'

'Why didn't you put it on Crusader's Horn? I thought you always went for horses from Malton stables.'

Father looked at me in a puzzled way.

'How did you know Crusader's Horn won?' he asked.

I knew that the cat was out of the bag, so I tipped out all my ill-gotten gains from the housekeeping purse and said, 'Will that help to recoup your loss?'

I was bidden not to tell mother. Secretly I think he was a teeny bit proud of me, and ever after that day he took note of my 'tips'.

When I became a vicar's wife I had to put away my gambling traits. Race going was not an option – yet strangely I spent my vicarage years folding raffle tickets and begging for tombola prizes. I have never been to a race meeting since I married, though temptation did get the better of me on a Mothers' Union outing to Chester. As I came out of the cathedral I saw crowds of exuberant ladies tottering around in high-heeled sandals and exposing much cleavage. It was Chester Races Ladies' Day. I missed my tea in the cathedral refectory in favour of standing on the city walls overlooking the Roodee racecourse and cheering on the outsider as the horses thundered passed me.

Looking up at Woolly I was less excited. What on earth had inspired us to give camping and boating a break and to go for a horse-drawn caravan holiday? Quite frankly I was terrified. This huge Welsh cob might kick. He might bite. He might trample on the children. He might trample on me! The man in charge gave us a crash course in harnessing the beast, and then watched as we tried to make sense of all the leatherwork. Crocheting was easier by comparison. I had never realised there were so many bits to put round and over and under. To be fair to Woolly he stood there patiently – probably groaning inwardly that it was Saturday again and the novices were at work on his head, on his back and belly and lastly pulling his tail through the crupper.

Half an hour later I realised that the harnessing had been the easy bit. The next stage was to get the horse to walk backwards into the shafts. Woolly saw the impending end to his freedom and decided to walk forwards and then, to evade capture, he galloped round the field with the farmer and all our family in hot pursuit. Eventually he was enticed with sugar lumps to calm him down while we surreptitiously brought the shafts ever nearer. Soon we were ready to take to the road, secure in the knowledge that the farmer would meet us by Llangorse lake the next morning to check that we had remembered every last bit of his harnessing lesson, and could be passed out to 'do the route' over the next six days.

The brown and yellow vardo bounced over the verge and onto the open road. Michael stayed close to Woolly's head and kept him on a tight rein. I held the dog and shepherded the three children along the country road. We were making for the nearest overnight stop, aware that we had to unharness in the correct order, tether the horse and then set about discovering the intricacies of the caravan. As we bumped our way into the field there was a crash. It had been a mistake to leave a large pan of stewed brambles on the cooker top. As I started to scoop up the mess and rack my brain as to what would get bramble stain out of a bit of fawn carpet I was somewhat cheered by Michael's announcement that the other family who had just arrived with their van in the field had suffered a worse disaster. Grandma had left the loo bucket untethered inside their van. Daughter-in-law was unhappy. We never saw them after that first night. Perhaps they went home.

Vicarages are usually large. Gypsy caravans are very small. We felt very cosy as we squashed up to have our tea and thought, 'What a wonderful life gypsies live!' The children then sat outside in the setting sun whittling twigs with penknives to try to make clothes pegs. I put on my Hungarian blouse, tied a scarf round my head and played folk songs on my guitar. Woolly munched contentedly; later we would look at our revision notes on harnessing. However, inside the van all was not well. Michael was trying to make up the beds at the rear. It was soon obvious that this was going to be a more time- consuming job than the harnessing. Fifty-eight minutes and several slipped discs later victory was declared. We collapsed into bed with the children and slept soundly until hailstones pounded on the canvas roof, the sky was ablaze with lightning, and thunder cracked, roared and rumbled for the next hour. I hoped that our rubber wheels would save us from being struck by lightning. Woolly decided to make a bolt for it, and in frantic fright uprooted his tethering stake and charged madly round and round the field.

At this point I would gladly have exchanged this holiday for a camping or a narrowboat one. Gypsies rose many notches higher in my estimation. How did they manage to keep their vans so neat and clean? Where did they dry their washing on rainy days? And more urgently, how did they catch their horse?

We learned a lot on that first night. We even gained 90% in our harnessing assessment the following morning. At the end of the week we were quite blasé about the whole process, had whittled the bed-making-up time to 29 minutes, and had stopped at every pub on the route – for the horse's crisps of course.

Two years later we repeated the experience, but this time in the Brecklands area of Norfolk, where we could make up our own route as long as we used certain night stops. It was Spring Bank Holiday week and the weather was superb. Passing motorists stopped to take photos and really did think we were gypsies – we were so tanned (and we like to think that we looked supremely confident with our horse, Jessie). On our penultimate afternoon we pulled into the overnight field behind a stream of BBC vans. Men with clipboards strode to the far end of the field to another gypsy holiday caravan, whose occupants had decided to strip naked and hose each other down with the farmer's hosepipe. At the approach of the BBC they ran screaming into their van and did not emerge until dark.

The men wandered back to our van and enquired what we were having for breakfast the next morning. When I said, 'Bacon and egg, mushrooms and fried bread,' they wrote it down in a little book and nodded sagely at each other.

'You'll do fine,' they said. 'Just what we wanted. Three children and a dog, and a really photogenic breakfast.'

I had hope that he had prefaced us with the photogenic bit. However we were thrilled to learn that they were filming for Cliff Michelmore's 'Holiday' programme and we were to be followed all morning, filmed and interviewed.

The minute they had gone I began to sort out what everyone would wear. The children, for the one time ever in their lives, wished to appear in matching clothes. The only snag was that I had yet to finish the third navy polo-necked sweater, as somewhere along our gypsy lanes I had lost my cable needle. Necessity is the mother of invention. I sat on the van steps using the last of the fading light, cabling with a twig, and then knitting the neck. Night fell. Rosemary would have to have a crew and not a polo neck.

The next day at 7 a.m. we meticulously tidied up the van in readiness for the film crew. It was to no avail. Their first request was that we made the interior look more lived in.

'Could you perhaps scatter pyjamas over the floor?'

The Lord answered my prayers that my yolks wouldn't break when I cracked five eggs into the frying pan, as the camera zoomed in. Then we were filmed outside on the grass. Normally verbose I was stunned into muteness when told to 'converse normally' and finished up saying inane things to the children as the cameras rolled. Michael then put on a fine display of horse-catching and harnessing, thereby giving viewers of the Holiday programme a false sense of how idyllic such a holiday would be.

The children, resplendent in matching sweaters, which they had needed in the early morning, were now peeling them off.

'You can't take them off!' yelled a lady with a clipboard. 'We've got to think of continuity.'

Two hours and many degrees hotter, the children were dissolving into grease spots. By now we were on the road. One man filmed Michael's legs as he walked alongside the horse. Another was on the van with me as I controlled the reins. He was trying to film the horse's rear as we clip-clopped through the Norfolk countryside. He suspended his camera towards Jessie's nether regions. Her tail went up and I knew what was imminent. I tried to tell the cameraman but he hushed me up, indicating that the sound was on. Jessie was a great one for sound effects – not that we ever heard them on the subsequent programme. I wonder if that camera ever recovered?

The following January our Holiday programme was to appear on TV. Unfortunately the time clashed with a big service for the Week of Prayer for Christian Unity, but we knew someone in the parish who had a video machine. Arrangements were made. However the good Lord intervened by sending a Pennine blizzard, which meant that the service was cancelled. Gathered around our black and white television set we watched and wondered if we really spoke with such Yorkshire accents. Others sat and wondered why on earth I was so cruel to my children, making them wear chunky polo necked sweaters on the hottest day of summer.

The clip of Michael's legs was deemed worthy enough to be the opening caption for each of the Holiday programmes of that series. They are very shapely legs and looked suitably manly and rugged with thick socks and walking boots. I was impressed that one of our former parishioners recognised them and rang to confirm that they were Michael's legs. It was Carol, who had holidayed with us in Aberdyfi many years earlier and been in the adjacent bed in the blood donation hall.

'I would know those legs anywhere,' she said.

But she didn't volunteer to join us on our next Romany holiday!

Chapter Fourteen

B ecause we had said nice things about the Norfolk Romany caravan hire company, and hence given them very valuable free advertising by way of our television appearance, they rewarded us with a substantially discounted holiday with them the following year.

Clergy income was, at that time, sufficiently low for us to qualify for Family Income Supplement. To their credit our children bore this stoically as they queued for their free school meal tickets and went with us to an office where cheap school uniforms were doled out – not always in the appropriate colours. Additional perks were free dental care and free prescriptions for Michael and me. The offer of a heavily discounted holiday was certainly not one to be passed by.

The following year we arrived at the Norfolk base and did not have to stay for the statutory harnessing lesson. We were given our horse and told that we could set off. We realised from the start that Bimbo was lively. By the second day we realised that we had been given the 'naughty' horse. He had already demolished the little two-man tent we had put up by the side of the caravan for the two older children. On the final evening we changed his description from 'naughty' to 'wicked'. We had tethered him, eaten our tea, and then all gone out for a walk. On our return there was no sign of our equine friend. Equine fiend would have been more precise. The gate of the field was closed, but a telltale broken halter hung on the tethering post. Bimbo must have jumped. But where to? Suddenly there was an alarming sound of pounding hooves. If we had been a minute later in our horse-search, the owner of the nearby allotment would have had glass shards in his cucumbers that summer. Bimbo was perilously close to the cold frame, but swerved to the left and headed for the orchard where his rope caught on a tree and we were able to recapture him. The next day we handed the criminal back to the hirers and jumped into our car before they could offer us another cut-price holiday.

Back in Halifax the congregation turned out in force the following Sunday. Michael was well known for weaving our adventures into his post-holiday sermons. The theme on this occasion was 'tethering' and was based on the Palm Sunday reading about finding a colt, the foal of an ass, tethered. We had to be sure of being tethered to the right person – namely Christ – for in his service is perfect freedom. Yet so many of us are tethered to unhealthy lifestyles, to addictions and to the lure of money, possessions and fame. The disciples were to tell the owner of the colt that 'the Lord has need of him'. So God will unleash us and free us to serve him in a particular way, when he has special need of us.

There is a world of difference between being tethered and being tied. Most of the year we were happy to serve our parishioners and be available to them in their times of need, sorrow, sickness, bereavement as well as in times of celebration. Yet there were times when we felt 'tied'. We lived in a tied house, with the knowledge that if Michael died in office then the family and I would have to move out fairly speedily and find somewhere to live. We were, of course, tied to the parish every weekend and every Christmas and Easter – all times when many people were on holiday. This we accepted fully as part of the job in which we had the privilege to be. It was when the dictates of the parish diary encroached more and more into our family life, to its detriment, that we determined to make sure that we always took full advantage of our three Sundays' holiday each year.

We also realised early in our ministry that it was no good planning a holiday based from home. It was essential to get right away from the doorbell and telephone. It was also essential to tell only our parents where we were going – otherwise there was the danger of being called back to take a funeral. We thought we had solved this problem by going camping and telling the flock that we didn't know where we would end up. One year we chose a site near Morecambe Bay. Feeling thoroughly liberated we ran into the sea, jumped waves and behaved in a childish fashion. As Michael lifted his bikini-clad wife out of the sea and chased her up the beach we were suddenly aware of loud handclapping from a line of onlookers leaning over the rails of the promenade.

'Well done vicar!' the women cried.

'Like your bikini!' shouted the men.

Fifty members of St. Jude's Darby and Joan Club were on their annual outing. They had caught up with the vicar and his wife and had photos to prove it. We prayed they would not be back home in time to print them in next month's parish magazine.

Canal holidays made us more elusive. We didn't know where we would be mooring each evening, and neither would anyone else. Similarly with Romany caravan holidays – our night stops were in the lap of the gods, or should I say at the whims of the horse. Yet not all our holidays were 'on the move'. We hired a caravan near New Quay on the Cardiganshire coast for several years running. Our children, brought up in large vicarages, absolutely loved the cosiness of a caravan. Now, in adulthood, they recall with pleasure the evening ritual of cuddling up on the bed while I read to them the story of 'Adventures of the Little Wooden Horse' by Ursula Moray Williams - one chapter each night. Each day we would drive to the beach and join in the Holiday Beach Mission activities. The children loved the stories, the competitions and the tugs-of-war, and we learned new choruses to teach the children who would come to our Halifax Holiday Club in the penultimate week of the summer holidays.

Although I had never wanted to be a teacher, and at this point had never taught in Sunday schools, I did enjoy helping to organise these Holiday Clubs, along with the neighbouring United Reformed church. We had an abundance of talented helpers and each year spent four intensive days working with fifty children aged from 5 to 11. The opening act of worship was based on a theme which we tried to carry over to the morning's activities. Over the years we did cooking – very popular with the boys – woodwork, stone carving, art straws, dance-drama, science, bug-hunts, origami and art. In the afternoons we went swimming, did treasure hunts, held sports and went on visits to tie in with our theme.

One year we gave the children the chance to learn about two contrasting ways of worship – with the Quakers and with the Serbian Orthodox Church. As a result of our contact with the latter, Michael and I were invited to celebrate the Orthodox Easter with them. This fell on the Sunday after our Easter; it was also on the day when we had to be back for the annual meeting of our parish – usually a lengthy and sometimes contentious affair.

After our own morning services at the hospital where Michael was chaplain, and at our church, we crossed Halifax to join in the Orthodox celebrations, complete with wonderful singing and dancing. We came out of the hall clutching brightly painted eggs, and as special guests were taken to the priest's house where we sat in a circle in his lounge and were given a bread bun and a tot of very strong spirit. Michael sat in the seat of honour as the priest went on to explain that the large bread bun on the crocheted cloth by the open door was to stay there from Easter day until the

Ascension, symbolic of Christ's time of appearances on earth to his disciples. All eyes went to the little table. All except Michael's. He dared not look at it, or at me, or especially at the priest. The large bun was not on the table. It was sitting heavily inside Michael's stomach. He had wrongly assumed that he had been allocated the large bun to consume along with the throat-burning spirit.

I expect that the priest's wife had to knock up another bun that evening. Meanwhile back at St. Jude's we had the shortest and jolliest annual general meeting on record. The spirit was certainly at work in Michael!

As well as holidays we did try to ensure we had a day off each week. It couldn't always be a Saturday, as weddings, fêtes and shows occurred generally on this day, but whenever possible we would try to keep Saturdays free to go out and about with the family. Living so far from the sea, yet loving to be on water, we bought a fibreglass dinghy, a bit like a floating bathtub, which we could transport on the car roof rack to nearby canals. Initially we rowed around in it, but later bought a small outboard motor. We christened the boat 'Jemima' and she came on seaside holidays with us too. The New Quay Beach Mission team was delighted. They could re-enact scenes on the Lake of Galilee using our boat – storms on the lake, and the miraculous draught of fishes.

Michael and Christopher would lift the boat up onto the roof rack at the end of the day and I lashed it on with blue nautical rope, once more calling upon my

Girl Guide knotting skills and executing a round turn and several half hitches. For years Jemima was transported safely from Yorkshire to Wales and Cornwall. Then Michael splashed out on a dedicated 'fasten your boat to a roof rack kit'. I had to admit that the procedure was greatly simplified, though I did miss doing my knots.

Returning from a holiday in Devon we decided to cross into Wales via the Severn Bridge. We were travelling in the slow lane when, about a quarter of the way across the bridge, I saw that Michael was gazing through his wing mirror and looking agitated.

'What's the matter?' I asked.

'We've lost the boat,' he croaked.

I opened my window and put up my hand to the roof. There was no boat. There had been a violent gust of wind, but we hadn't seen the boat take off. We presumed it must have done and that it was now lying many yards below in the River Severn. We couldn't stop on the bridge as we were in a line of holiday traffic, but parked as soon as we could and walked back across the bridge in search of the boat.

'Have you lost anything, sir?' asked the waiting policeman.

'Yes,' said Michael, 'we've lost our boat.'

I stifled my laughter when I realised that the police thought it a serious offence. It was. The boat had been blown into the air and onto the opposite carriageway landing on the bonnet of a carload of unsuspecting holidaymakers on their way home to London after a hitherto peaceful holiday in Wales. Luckily they were unhurt, but can you imagine their insurance claim?:

'We were driving south on the Severn Bridge, when suddenly a flying boat approached us at an angle of 45 degrees.'

Having collected our car from the Welsh end of the bridge, we had to drive back into England, retrieve our wrecked shell of a boat, strap it onto the roof rack (yes, I knew my knotting skills would be valuable once more) and return home via Gloucestershire. We tried to find a tip where we could off-load Jemima, but Council tips are about as elusive as the holiday venues of the Walker family, and we made the return journey with the passenger side window open and my arm up on the roof rack to reassure the ashen-faced children that the boat was still in place.

The story had a happy ending. The manufacturers of the boat clips admitted a faulty design. The uprush of the gusty wind had expanded the inside of the fibreglass boat and caused the clips to pop off. With the generous insurance payment we were able to buy a small wooden cabin cruiser. By now we had moved to serve in the Church in Wales and our vicarage had the Llangollen canal running right behind it.

This boat, 'Cwch Bach' meaning 'little boat', served us well for several years. We rarely used it for holidays, as it slept only two officially, but it was a real bolt-hole. We could escape from the phone for an hour or two, chug along the Dee Valley, have tea, and return refreshed for the evening meeting. We also used it as extra sleeping accommodation in Llangollen Eisteddfod week, when the vicarage was filled with folk singers and dancers from Lithuania, Hungary, Portugal, Denmark and Norway. When all on our multinational guest list had been given supper and were in bed, Michael and I would creep out and climb up the towpath, jump down onto the boat and into the waiting sleeping bags.

Wooden boats require much maintenance. While I was happy to sit on the boat and read, or write, or chat to passers-by, Michael seemed to spend his time trying to stem the leaks. He tried various ways of patching and water-repelling. The cabin became a repository for failed tins and tubes of sealants. One cold April afternoon we went up to the boat to try out an impressive plastic syringe full of foam that would fill the cracks.

'Margaret,' came the shout from the cabin, 'can you come down and move the table leg so that I can get at the floorboard?'

As I grovelled under the table Michael started to apply his syringe. In the semi-gloom he couldn't see that it was pointing to my head. I screamed. Michael scrambled out of the cabin, lowered a bucket into the canal and threw the water at my head as he thought the foam could be toxic so should be washed off as speedily as possible.

The effect, of course, was not to remove the foam but to set it solidly on the left-hand side of my head.

Water-repellent it certainly proved to be. I ran back home and hoped, vainly, that hot water and shampoo would be the answer. My hair was encased in an unyielding white cast. I knew that it would have to be cut off. I applied my dressmaking shears, then looked in the mirror. You might think that I didn't know whether to laugh or to cry. I can tell you; I cried. Michael persuaded me to go straight to Irene, the hairdresser. She took one look at me, and as she reached for her scissors I knew my fate was sealed. She had to cut off the hair at the other side to make it match. Then she had to shorten the back. I was scalped. This was also the day I was wearing spectacles for the first time. I looked like a cartoon character.

I went back home and ate my tea miserably. I would have to stay away from the public eye for a week or two, or at least wear a hat whenever I went out. Michael suggested I found a hat straightaway. The S4C television team was filming that night in our church for 'Dechrau Canu, Dechrau Canmol', the Welsh equivalent of 'Songs of Praise'. I had completely forgotten about this, but I was needed to sing alto. Thank goodness the altos would be behind the sopranos, and I would be far away from the camera.

Luck was not on my side that day. The producer decided that she wanted the altos on the front row. Then she cast her eyes around the congregation and noticed that some were wearing hats.

'It's better if you all take your hats off,' she said. 'We don't want to give the impression that church-goers are old-fashioned.'

I cringed as I peeled off my 'safety helmet' of a woolly hat.

'I didn't see you on that Welsh hymn singing programme,' said friends from other parishes when they phoned me. 'We saw all the other members of the choir. You've got a new lady haven't you – the one at the front in big glasses and with an odd hairstyle. Has she got a good voice?'

'Not really,' I replied. 'But I'm sure you'll like her!'

Chapter Fifteen

Exposing my shaved head on television to thousands of viewers was embarrassing, but nothing to compare with my knickers falling down in front of the Archbishop.

It was in the 1960s, the era of the miniskirt, when Michael and I were invited back to York for the dedication of St. Mark's, the new church on the housing estate where Michael had served his first curacy. We had helped to hammer in the stakes marking the site and seen the arrival of the first bricks. Now we were proud to be included in the guest list for the special service for the opening of this dual-purpose building.

As we moved up the queue in the entrance way to shake hands with Dr Donald Coggan, Archbishop of York, the elastic in my knickers snapped. To stop their descent I hastily put my knees together, but was immediately propelled forward in the line-up. The Archbishop gave me a most puzzled gaze as I minced my way towards him with a knock-kneed gait.

'Hello Margaret. Are you well?' he asked.

'Yes, very well, thank you,' I replied.

He did not look convinced. As I shuffled onwards I felt his gaze on my oddly aligned legs. Michael forestalled further enquiries by taking over the conversation with His Grace, while I sought out the Ladies lavatory and proceeded to kick off the offending garment and stuff it into my handbag.

I had hoped to grab a serviette, a plate and a cucumber sandwich and merge into the throng in the hall. But fate decreed that Michael and I were to climb up onto the stage to sit at the guest table with the Archbishop and Mrs Coggan. This was not a happy position to be in for a knickerless curate's wife. Michael shared my welling embarrassment and with great presence of mind seated me at the far side of the table and surreptitiously pulled down the front of the tablecloth to act as my safety shield. I was soon conversing animatedly with Mrs Coggan. I was with her on a later occasion at a Clergy Wives' conference at Scargill House in Wharfedale, where I learned that despite an austere upbringing she had a lively sense of humour. She chortled with obvious relish when I revealed the 'naked truth'!

She led our bible studies brilliantly and gave us younger clergy wives a great deal of sensible advice and encouragement. One thing that she told us I have never forgotten. It has proved to be of inestimable use in bible study groups. It was the mnemonic for remembering the order of some of Paul's epistles and came from her teetotal background:

Get Every Pub Closed. Brilliant for finding your way speedily to Galatians, Ephesians, Philippians and Colossians and a sure-fire way to impress at a clergy gathering.

I had always relied on mnemonics to get me through exams. From learning the compass points by Never Eating Shredded Wheat, I progressed to an extremely lengthy one of my own making which spanned the entire gamut of the French Revolution. My favourite was one I invented for Disraeli's home reforms. Mention Disraeli to me now and I can smell the odour of sweaty feet in my Girl Guide tent, leading me to remember the word CAMPFEET. I could not believe my luck when one of my history 'O' level questions was on Disraeli's home reforms. I rattled off paragraphs on Climbing boys, Artisans' dwellings, Merchant shipping, Public health, Factories, Enclosure of commons, Education and Trade unions, which went a long way towards the 85% I was duly awarded.

Our history teacher passed this word on to succeeding generations; for all I know CAMPFEET are still walking around the corridors of Beverley High School. I wonder if she also passed on to them that incredibly useful rhyme about the order of kings and queens of England: Willy, Willy, Harry Ste... ending William and Mary, Anna Gloria, four Georges, William and Victoria. For homework we had to make a rhyme for the subsequent monarchs. Mine can't have been memorable so it's a good job I know the 20th century ones anyway. The only snag with this rhyme is that when a question on monarchs crops up on Mastermind the contestant has relinquished his chair before I have chanted my aide-mémoire, reached the appropriate point, and shouted out 'Henry the Sixth.' in an effort to impress my family.

Teaching methods and educational policies have moved on apace since my schooldays, which began with writing on slates, gardening for wartime, and paying tuppence-ha'penny a week for daily bottles of milk. These chubby milk bottles were left out in the playground, next to the smelly outdoor toilets. In the summer the milk would be rancid, or at best have creamy lumps floating around, and in the winter the milk would freeze and push off the cardboard tops. These were avidly collected, as they were excellent for winding wool round to make pom-poms to adorn our hats.

At junior school we had daily religious instruction, along with arithmetic and English. We had to do high jump on an asphalt playground with no landing mats. Maybe that was why we also had First Aid on our curriculum. The deputy head, Miss Ross, was small and rotund and a keen member of the St. John Ambulance Brigade. I enjoyed her First Aid lessons until we came to do artificial respiration. She needed a model on which to demonstrate. I volunteered and had to lie, stomach downwards, across two desks. As Miss Ross applied pressure to the small of my back she inadvertently pushed the two desks together, thereby pinching my tummy and inflicting on it two impressive striped bruises.

What with a punctured abdomen and a pea-souper of a fog on the day of the 11+ exam it was a wonder I made it to High School. There the first year girls were put in prefab classrooms and split alphabetically. I can still go right through the register of Upper 3B: Jackson, Jefferson, Longbone, Luke... it was our morning and afternoon mantra. Miss Davies, our headmistress, told us in her opening address that whereas Bridlington High School went in for brains, Beverley High School turned out 'Ladies'. At the end of each term, after the reading of everyone's exam percentages, came the Deportment list and the Courtesy list. I had to rely on being well up on the first list; I both slouched and refused to grovel to the mistresses, begging to carry their books, so Margaret Jefferson never appeared in lights on the latter two lists.

Looking back I can see what a misguided system there was for predetermining our career paths. On the basis of the first year exam results alone, we were split into four groups for the rest of our school life up to the Fifth Form. Those achieving the first eight places in the overall percentages were to do Latin, the next twenty to study German, those lower down the list to do science and those at the bottom to do cookery. Because my own children between them did maths, chemistry, physics, biology and technical drawing I managed to fill in a few scientific gaps, and Michael is eternally grateful that my mother and sister inculcated culinary skills into me. A pre-university trip to work in a refugee camp in Austria and later a friendship with Swiss-Germans enabled me to 'get by' in German, so, all things considered, I look back with gratitude that I was chosen at the age of eleven to do Latin. Through it I learned more English language than ever I did in

English lessons and it has formed a useful basis for understanding Spanish, Portuguese and Italian.

Physical education took the form of hockey and netball in winter, cricket, tennis and athletics in summer, and dancing and gym all year round. I loathed most of these, but hated hockey with a vengeance. Why should I have to stand on a muddy pitch near the east coast, with winds blowing from the Ural Mountains, dressed only in an Aertex blouse and navy knickers, to be whacked on the shins by hearty stick-wielders in search of a hard white ball? I prayed for rain each Wednesday and Friday. When God obliged I then had to go on bended knee again to ask that the PE mistress would decide on dancing or gym as an alternative, and not subject us to a test on hockey rules, about which I had no understanding whatsoever. A badly sprained ankle in the fourth form was strangely prolonged to get me out of hockey for the whole season. That was the first time in which I received a positive report under 'Sport' at the end of term. During my sixth form years I ingratiated myself with the PE staff by volunteering to work in the school canteen on Saturday mornings preparing sandwiches for the visiting hockey teams. Our home team brought a mishmash of ingredients, which we put together with ingenuity - corned beef and carrot, cucumber and pilchards, cream cheese with strawberry jam. Excellent training for a future vicar's wife!

Geography was a sensible subject, covering every continent, teaching me about map projections, alternative sources of energy, and most usefully – how to read a map. The fact that I had a 'crush' on the geography teacher may have influenced my liking for the subject, but she gave me a lifelong love of maps. Even today with our powerful GPS navigation aids in the car it is gratifying that Michael will sometimes listen to 'the little lady in the passenger seat' in preference to 'the electronic lady' who panics if he takes a detour and implores him in an American accent to 'please turn back!'

Maths, French, scripture, music and English language presented no problems. English literature did. An uninspiring teacher and the introduction to Shakespeare at too early an age killed all desire to read the classics. I am unenthusiastically still catching up. With a great deal more enthusiasm I am catching up on art. My first term report stymied teenage artistic effort. It read, 'Art – drawing is only very fair, and Margaret's use of paint is poor because she scrubs.' In an effort to inspire me, my brother-in-law bought me a book on art. I was determined to work my way through it and end up as a Rembrandt or a Rubens. I only managed to get as far as page 2, where there was an exercise on drawing a pig. This I practised for hours. I can do it now. Only a left-facing pig, however, and only one standing in tufts of grass, thereby eliminating the need to draw its trotters. From that day on I proceeded to introduce a pig into every art exam. Whereas other people had houses with pretty gardens, I had farms with pigs. At the zoo I introduced no elephants or giraffes, just pigs. When the topic was 'A butcher's shop' my heart leapt. I drew my left-hand facing pigs hanging downwards from butchers' hooks, and avoided drawing the butcher's features by having just his belly, complete with blue and white striped apron, protruding from the edge of the page. I came second in art that year. All that remained was for me to do well in a needlework exam.

It was hard being a tailor's daughter. Everyone expected you to be able to sew. It was even harder when your sister was brilliant at sewing. Luckily the first year project was embroidery and I didn't mind this. We were to design and make up 'needlework aprons' in which to keep our accessories. I was completely carried away with an intricate design that included a tape measure, scissors and many bobbins of cotton. I would have simplified this had I known that we were also to embroider, in chain stitch, our full name along the bottom. Ann Bell used to be my friend. Not after the first term. She had finished her minimalist design and name, and had progressed to making a pair of shorts. Two terms later I had finished embroidering every quarter inch mark on my tape-measure, and had started the arduous stitching journey of 'Dorothy Margaret Jefferson'.

Down-sizing to a small cottage in retirement I parted with piles of my essay books, artwork, and school reports but I carefully folded and stowed away in a drawer that needlework apron, and wondered whether Ann Bell still had hers. They are relics of bygone days with a rapidly receding language of hedge-tear darns, bias binding edging, blanket stitch and faggoting.

I know I am getting old when I see articles like darning mushrooms appear on 'Antiques Roadshow'.

'What's darning, Grandma?'

'It's what we did in the war, dear. I don't think you'll ever need to know how to do it.

'Or if you do, please don't ask grandma to show you. Just come and tell me if you have a hole in your socks and I'll give you a pound to buy some new ones!

'However if you want help with quadratic equations, Disraeli's home reforms or conjugating French verbs - je suis ici!'

Chapter Sixteen

'Achtung!' I yelled, as the Austrian stationmaster locked me into a wire cage on the platform of Bischofshofen station.

'Achtung!' warned Herr Grüber, as I tripped up on the edge of his cement pit.

I was 18 and full of idealistic plans to improve the lot of the world's poor. My headmistress had curbed my intent to leap into missionary activity in India and suggested that I might first study social science. I was accepted to do this at Nottingham University starting in October 1958. In between school and university I had signed up to go out to work on a refugee camp in Austria under the auspices of the United Nations. A group of boys and I, from the church youth fellowship, planned to be driven out there in a converted ambulance by Michael's father's new curate.

Plans fell apart. The curate developed appendicitis, the ambulance proved not to be roadworthy, and the boys backed out when their doting parents discovered that TB was rife on the camp. My father, a survivor of the horrors of the First World War, was not going to let stories of TB intimidate his daughter from going out to help Yugoslav refugees build houses of their own and escape from years of living in huts on encampments which had little sanitation.

I travelled alone to London Victoria where I met the other volunteers. I was placed with Katherine and James, undergraduates from Oxford.

'You three have the longest journey,' said a harassed looking organiser. 'Here are your tickets – to Wagna, by way of Graz. You should get there in about 38 hours time.'

If my legs ever appear to have a criss-cross pattern on them, it's not from wearing fishnet tights. It's a relic of a night trying to sleep on a net luggage rack as our train rattled through Western Europe.

We had to change trains at Bischofschofen, in Austria, but between trains we had the prospect of a welcome freshen-up in a nearby swimming pool. Our luggage, we were assured, would be safe if we left it on the platform. Someone would lock it in a huge cage. I was partway down the path to the pool when I realised I hadn't brought a towel with me, so ran back to get one out of my case. CLICK. The stationmaster hadn't seen me crouching behind the pile of cases on towel-retrieving duty. I was locked inside the cage like a monkey. At least monkeys have onlookers. I was alone – the station suddenly strangely deserted. Then that magic word, which I'd seen on train notices and heard in station announcements, sprang into my head.

'Achtung, achtung!' I bellowed, as I rattled the cage like a deranged ape.

They let me out, of course. I had a swim and we all progressed to Graz. It was dark when we changed trains again onto an old boneshaker with wooden slatted benches. Katherine and James and I had taken it in turns to sleep, with one of us on 'looking out duty' to ensure that we didn't miss our stop. It was on the last leg of the journey that I was on watch. We stopped at one station; it seemed to be called HERREN. Through the gloom and flickering station lights the next began with DAM... As we jolted to a halt at another stop my companions woke up and gazed out blearily.

'Aren't we there yet?'

'No, we're at HERREN-DAMEN' I replied, thinking it was a posh double-barrelled name like Lyme Regis or Tunbridge Wells.

Once again it was 'Achtung!' time as I shouted to the guard who was about to wave the train off. He helped us off with our cases and we stood in a huddle feeling like a trio of evacuees with no one to meet them.

My knowledge of German was increasing fast. Now I knew three words: Attention, Gents and Ladies. Keep this up and I'd be fluent by the time I drew my pension. The longest word I had to learn was flüchtlingslager – refugee camp. My next challenge was to try to find our way through a mass of wooden huts to our accommodation. It was 2 a.m. and very dark. It was a shame they hadn't told us to bring a torch. There was a light high up in the distance; we decided to aim for that. We processed in the manner of three wise men looking up at the guiding star. Our cases were heavy. We too were bearing gifts – presents for the refugee families from the local United Nations groups at home. Our eyelids were heavy too. We didn't speak; 800 refugees were asleep. At least they were until I tripped. A gaggle of geese resented disturbance to their pen and set off an alarming goose-equivalent of 'Achtung!' Lights went on, curtains twitched, torches beamed on us. Never fear. We are here. Courtesy of the United Nations Aid to Refugees.

The light we were following proved to be the administration block and below it was the volunteers' hut. We crept inside. I was determined to slink silently onto my palliasse and cause no further disturbance. Only as I pulled out my pyjamas did I remember that, round the edge of the case, my sister had packed tubes of Rollos, Polos, Rowntrees fruit gums and everything that could roll, as presents for the refugee children. Out they sprang and rolled noisily all over the wooden floor. The disturbed volunteers seemed to know quite a few words far more venomous than 'Achtung'. I was to remember them on the day I fell into the cement pit during a thunderstorm. The German language is more expressive than English in such situations.

To begin with I was put on cooking duty. We had to be up at 4.30 a.m. to light the wood-burning stove on which to make porridge, and then to paste oily margarine onto dense, dark-brown rye bread. Onto this was spread the welcome addition of superb apricot jam – America's contribution marked 'aid to refugees'. It is still my favourite jam.

I didn't do many stints on cooking duty. Maybe it was because of the frankfurters.

I had been sent to town with Marcelle who came from Bradford. She was 17 and the only volunteer younger than me. We thought we'd been sent to buy 20 kilos of frankfurters. Apparently they had said 20 frankfurters. It took us two journeys with severe back strain to carry them back to camp. We had used up a considerable portion of the kitchen budget; the frankfurters had to be consumed.

Meal number one – frankfurters and reconstituted mashed potatoes – was a resounding success. The addition of frankfurters to the minimal breakfast of porridge and rye bread provoked further cheers. Meal number three posed a problem. How were we to disguise yet more of the wretched sausages? Marcelle and I were not born in Yorkshire for nothing. Eggs, milk and flour were available.

'Hurray,' they cried. 'Yorkshire pudding.'

Only as they dug deeper did they find the ingeniously hidden frankfurters masquerading as 'Toad in the hole'.

On the fourth meal we did succeed with our deception. Cutting the sausage skins, I scraped out the meat, mixed it with rye breadcrumbs and porridge oats and fried it as rissoles, served with the unusually sweet accompaniment of apricot jam. It was a triumph. I never divulged the secret recipe. I made a mental note to add Flüchtlinslager Frankfurters to my already best-selling 'Cucumber and Swarfega sandwiches' and 'Margaret's million meals with mince'.

Despite my long awaited culinary success I was put on building duty for the rest of the month, working from 5.30 a.m. to 1 p.m. when it became too hot to stay on site. I mixed cement, heaved breeze-blocks and trundled wheelbarrows. At 9 a.m. we had a break for rye bread and a very acidic cold drink. As we shared it round I thought it looked like a mini Communion service. When I first tasted the sour wine I had even more sympathy for Jesus at Golgotha. Surely this was the same stuff they had offered to him, soaked on a sponge. Like him I rejected it. I hope my refusal didn't offend the Grüber family whose house I was helping to build. All the family – herrens, damens, kinder and grandparents – slaved daily in an effort to speed on their house building and the moving out from the long, low wooden huts where they had been interned for many years. It was a humbling experience to help them.

The sanitation on the camp was dire – far worse than my Girl Guide latrines. Flimsy sacking hardly hid the slimy yellow-ochre mud trenches into which you were prone to slither after rainstorms. Tight nose-pinching could not staunch the stench. Constipation seemed a safer option.

I returned from Wagna constipated, tanned and with a much greater understanding of the continuing aftermath of war. I had also passed my apprenticeship as a breeze-block layer, and added useful words like sand, gravel and spade to my vocabulary.

Forty years on and I had learned a few more German words, thanks to a wonderful friendship with a Swiss family as a result of a chance encounter that Michael and Christopher had with Jack – a Swiss engine driver - on one of their railway holidays. I can still recall the surprise of Jack and his wife Ursula when one evening I casually brought into the conversation the word flüchtlingslager.

That night I dreamed about the refugee camp. The more I thought about it the more I wondered what had happened to families like the Grübers. What was Wagna like now? Well, there was one way to find out. Search for it on the Internet. Far from being a hamlet based on an old campsite it was now a dormitory area of Leibnitz. A few clicks of the mouse later and I had a plan. I would go back and see it for myself – only this time I would go away with the vicar.

Chapter Seventeen

The heavy metal cell door slammed shut and we climbed into our hospital-type, single cot-like beds. The last glimmer of sunshine threw the shadows of the window bars onto the white counterpane. That night it was no surprise that I dreamed of refugees, prisoners, huts and latrines.

I had never slept in a prison cell before. Neither had I thought of travelling to Austria by way of Slovenia. Michael, never one to do a simple trip if there was a more complicated and scenic rail journey to be done, decided we should fly out to Ljubljana, take the train over the border, visit Wagna, stay overnight in Graz, and then resume our Slovenian holiday at Lake Bohinj. Where should we stay in Ljubljana? Our young Slovenian friend, Manca, suggested Hostel Celista, near the railway station. As we approached the location we were sure she had misdirected us and that we were at the wrong place. The encompassing walls were covered with graffiti and it looked more like a prison. We were right. It was! At least it had been.

By night it was a Youth Hostel; by day it was a tourist attraction, and in the afternoons visitors were allowed to peer into the cells, which now also doubled as an art gallery, with each cell ceiling decorated by a different artist. At the modern reception area we were welcomed warmly, given our keys and a conducted tour – a well-appointed café, a quiet space, and a room where some were smoking hubble-bubble pipes. I was relieved to find modern showers and toilets, as I had noted that the red-tiled corridor floor sloped to a central gully, where I presumed the prisoners used to slop out.

Despite the heavy doors and small barred window I did not feel claustrophobic. The ceiling was very high and the air was fresh. As I gazed up at the night sky I recalled the lines about two men looking from prison bars, and one seeing mud, the other stars. I saw stars, and hoped that I would be led, as I was 44 years ago, to the site of the refugee huts.

My Internet perusals bore fruit. The train left Ljubljana at 8.30 a.m. and we changed at Maribor, arriving in Leibnitz to catch one of the very infrequent buses to Wagna. We hadn't a clue where to get off on this sprawling estate of bungalows. One of them might have been Herr Grüber's house, standing proudly on my breeze-blocks! But there was no landmark; nothing on the horizon that gave me any indication of my bearings. In truth I was already feeling a sense of anti-climax. Why had I come back? To dismount from a little bus into an anonymous housing estate to indulge in nostalgia?

Sensing my disappointment, Michael steered me into a café for a cup of coffee. From a door in the only block of flats on the estate came an elderly couple who sat at the next table and seemed to be ordering lunch.

'Austrian cheap lunch for pensioners' day,' said Michael. 'Do you think we would qualify?'

I didn't answer. I was immersed in my own thoughts. Then I looked at the couple and decided – it's now or never. I doubted if they would understand English, so I wrote on my serviette 'Flüchtlingslager – 1958', took it over to them and proceeded to do a charade of mixing cement and trundling wheelbarrows. They looked bewildered, but when I pointed across the road, squatted, held my nose, and said 'pooh' they looked at each other knowingly and indicated that I must stay, while the man ran off to his nearby flat.

He returned three minutes later bearing two ring-bound files full of documents and pictures of him and his wife, Thérèse, on the refugee camp. With increasing excitement we communicated with odd words of German and English, and much acting. He was an Austrian, and he had married Thérèse, a Serbian, who had been in the camp from 1943 to 1961. Her father had been a doctor and she was trained as a children's nurse. I brought out my photos, with the administrative block in the background. It was three storeys high; so was the block of flats behind us. I was here, having coffee on the site of the volunteers' hut, and, yes, I had pointed in the exact direction of the smelly latrines.

'We must have a photo of all this,' said Michael. He was right. It was a memorable occasion. Thérèse, now

82 and rather frail, put her arms round me and kissed me.

'Danke, danke,' she cried, as tears welled up in her eyes, then in mine, and then in the eyes of the menfolk.

It had been right to make this journey. Sometimes you should look back.

Chapter Eighteen

When our children look back at their childhood it is gratifying that they all recall happy holidays. But among cosy memories of boats, caravans, camping and beaches they all hark back to Hither Green.

Every family adds unique words or phrases to its vocabulary.

'Look out, mum and dad are going to have a Hither Green,' warns Christopher, as Michael and I have a disagreement and start raising our voices. How did this area of south-east London come into our family phraseology?

It was a long journey to our holiday cottage in Lydd in Kent. The red Morris Marina estate car was loaded early on the Saturday morning: two adults, three children, Sheba dog, buckets and spades, cases, books, games, boxes of food and a picnic. The journey was, as usual, punctuated by stops near railway locations. I know most sidings and depots in the UK and can direct you to the backsides of Carnforth, Doncaster and Swindon, and to most narrow-gauge railways, without so much as a glance at a map. Pauline, Rosie, Sheba and I were baled out in North London with instructions to be back at the same roundabout in two hours time. Michael and Christopher drove off to explore Willesden and Old Oak Common engine sheds. We had two hours in which to trudge round the hot July pavements.

Weary, warm and worn, we waited at the pre-arranged roundabout, and amid the hooting of cars behind us we jammed ourselves into the car among toppling piles of luggage. Michael, hot and cross, slammed the tailgate down hurriedly – unfortunately catching the tip of Shebas's tail. We drove on with the poor dog frantically wafting her bloody tail and showering droplets of blood onto the white roof of the car. There was blood at my feet too. It was not from the dog. It was oozing from the glove compartment. What had possessed me to stow away the liver for tonight's meal in the glove compartment? It was defrosting fast, and already I knew it would not be safe to cook it for tonight's dinner – that was if we ever got as far as Lydd.

My mood deteriorated further when Michael announced that he wanted to stop at Hither Green to 'do the sheds'. We had left home at 6.30 a.m. It was now 5 p.m. and all I wanted to do was to get to the cottage, unpack, eat and go to bed. I would have to cook egg and chips for speed.

'Don't be more than half an hour,' I called after Michael. 'I'll just pop in the shop on the corner and buy some potatoes.'

'Potatoes? Why on earth haven't you packed potatoes? You silly woman.'

To be reprimanded for the simple omission of potatoes was one thing. To be called a silly woman was another. To have this epithet hurled at me in the presence of Saturday afternoon shoppers in Hither Green was the end. The camel's back broke with a snap.

'How dare you call me a silly woman! Do you know what I did for you yesterday? I did the washing and the ironing. I packed all the cases, baked a fruit loaf and spent half an hour looking for your snorkel.'

I was now in full flow and my voice rose an octave as I continued: 'I typed the July parish magazine. I made a poster for the fête. I dealt with the woman who wanted to look at the parish registers, and sorted out wedding music for September's bride.'

I still had plenty of verbal ammunition left and I kept up a steady rant, stamping my feet to accentuate my rage.

Hell hath no fury like a woman scorned. Hither Green in 1981, the summer of Brixton riots and burned out cars, had to contend with me in full flow. How dare he call me a silly woman! Customers came out of the corner shop, curtains were pulled back and people came out onto their doorsteps to observe the Saturday evening riot.

The children stood by the car, wide-eyed at this hitherto unknown temper being displayed by their normally placid mother. Michael stood there laughing.

'You're quite splendid when you're mad,' he said. 'Come on, let's get down to Lydd and pick up fish and chips on the way.'

Worn out with the journey and my outburst I sank into the car. Michael threw away the stinking liver. We never did add potatoes to our holiday groceries. But we did add a new 'Walker expression'.

When one of Pauline's friends asked, 'Don't your mum and dad ever have a row?' she replied,

'Oh, yes, in 1981 they had a 'Hither Green'.

Maybe I should have gone in for more mini-'Hither Greens' back home in the vicarage. Instead I had gone along the biblical road of 'turning the other cheek' in the face of verbal attack. Just when things seemed to be going well there would be an upsetting phone call or a murmuring at the back of church. I can look back now and see how trivial the issues were, but at the time they 'got to me'. There was the newcomer to Llangollen who ranted and raved about the church bells ringing on a Sunday morning and shortening his lie in. He had just had a new bungalow built and was going to prosecute the vicar for allowing this disturbance of his peace. Of course I should have pointed out that there had been a church on that site since the sixth century, and that if he wanted peace and quiet he should have had his bungalow built elsewhere; but in the face of the threat of prosecution such reasoned arguments don't trip off the tongue.

Then there were the rabbits in the graveyard. They were eating the flowers off the graves. What were we to do? Some took the law into their own hands and went round with shotguns. Result – animal rights protestors storming the vicarage.

'Dig a trench round the cemetery and put ginger in it,' was one suggestion. Rather costly, we thought, and not a proven solution. We left the rabbits with a right to roam.

Returning from a Mothers' Union outing to Worcester we found Michael's mother dying on our front room settee. His father had sent for the doctor, but ten minutes later she was dead. The phone rang and I ran to answer it, thinking it might be the ambulance. It was not.

'I want to speak to the vicar.'

'I'm sorry, but it's not convenient just at the moment...'

'I know he's in – I saw you come back from the trip. Tell him to get to the phone NOW.'

'I'm sorry, he isn't free to come at the moment. Can I take a message?'

'Yes you can – tell him he's a disgrace. He hasn't done a thing about those rabbits. Do you know what they've done? They've eaten all the carnations off my mother's grave. I want to speak to him now.'

'I'm sorry about the carnations, but you can't speak to him now. His mother died five minutes ago.'

'I don't care about his b★★★★★ mother...'

I put down the phone and sobbed.

We carried many other similar scenarios in our hearts - other people's 'Hither Greens'. Twice a year we really needed to get away from the vicarage, to get life back in proportion and to return refreshed for the demanding but varied and rewarding work with our congregations and parishioners. We couldn't let rabbits stop us proclaiming the Good News!

Most of the time I was aware that our position carried with it many privileges, not least the warm welcome we invariably received when we moved to a new parish. Other people have described how lonely they felt when moving to a new town. We, on the other hand, arrived with a fanfare, to bouquets of welcome from the churchwardens, and to a house newly scrubbed by the Mothers' Union. After an inspiring induction and institution service we adjourned to a prolific buffet in the church hall, with tables sagging under the weight of Mrs Wilson's best chocolate sponge cake, Mrs Jones's Welsh cakes, and platefuls of sandwiches in which, mercifully, salmon had ousted the wartime potted meat.

Everyone knew us from the start. All we had to do was to smile and try to file away faces, names and addresses in our memory banks.

After each arrival in a new parish we were aware that, as the psalmist said, 'Our lot had been set in a fair ground. We had a goodly heritage.' We also took to heart the words, 'to whom much is given, much is expected.'

In York, Hull, Halifax, Llangollen and finally Kerry, in mid-Wales we made many good friends. We even took a coach load on holiday with us! Despite all the holiday stories they had heard from us, thirty-four people from our final deanery dared to venture forth with us on a pilgrimage to the Holy Land. The journey had an ominous start when, halfway to Heathrow, there was a large bang and smell of burning rubber. We had a police escort to the nearest service station. We needed a change of wheel, but we couldn't risk being late for our check-in. Another coach pulled in and nobly rescued us. We counted our 34 fellow pilgrims on, and ten days later counted them all back.

It was a big responsibility looking after so many people, ensuring that they were happy with their accommodation, that dietary requirements were being met, and that they realised the danger of pickpockets at the biblical sites. There were the mundane things like crossing 34 people over busy roads, finding toilets in the middle of Nazareth and searching for the one who got lost in the Ladies, and trying to keep everyone together on the Via Dolorosa. This was not the long straight road that I had imagined, but a series of narrow alleys, lined with shopkeepers intent on luring scripture-weary pilgrims into their tourist traps.

The pilgrimage proved to be a wonderful experience, with the gospel stories turning from the black and white print in our bibles into the living colours of Galilee, Nazareth and Jerusalem. We sang 'O Sabbath rest by Galilee. O calm of hills above…' as our little boat dropped anchor in the middle of the lake, and 'Blessed are the pure in heart' as we celebrated communion at 8 a.m. on the Mount of Beatitudes the next morning.

It was a time of blessing for us all. Two of our 34 pilgrims have since been ordained, three have become Readers, and two have become Worship leaders. We hope that they and all the others were glad that they took the risk of going away with the vicar.

Chapter Nineteen

Our children didn't always holiday with us; they went off on Brownie weekends, Guide camps, Diocesan pilgrimages and schemes where they learned to sail boats, build steps through forests and save the environment. We didn't really worry about them while they were away, although we did once receive a postcard smeared with blood, which read, 'I'm writing this in the doctor's surgery with my left hand. My right thumb is stuck in the top of a broken pop bottle. Having a great time, love Christopher.'

Maybe we did worry a little bit.

However, I think our children worried a great deal more about us when, after they had fled the nest, we took off on adventurous holidays, more often than not in Eastern Europe. We have never communicated with family by phone when we've been away. Only on our return from various holidays did they learn that we had been walking in a Romanian wood just a couple of hours after a man had been mutilated by a bear, and that we had ridden on donkeys down to Hatshepsut's temple just before several tourists had been shot at and killed. They were alarmed that we had parasailed above the Aegean Sea without extra insurance and were intrigued to know why we had been thrown out of a Greek Orthodox church for misbehaving.

I knew that it was not done to wear shorts in their churches, or to expose too much flesh. Suitably dressed, with a scarf over my head and long trousers to cover Michael's knees, we joined in the worship at a church on Halkidiki. As expected, their service was very different from ours, but we tried to stand up in the right places. Ten minutes into the service I realised that the men were at one side and the women at the other. Mistake number one on our part. Then I noticed that it was only the elderly or infirm who sat down. Mistake number two.

A verger-type man was sorting candles while the service progressed – tossing spent ones into a distant box, and ripping open cartons of new ones. He kept glowering at me; maybe it was because I had given him a hard stare for making so much noise. Equally distracting was the middle-aged lady, dressed in black, who appeared half an hour into the service bearing the Greek equivalent of Windolene. She sprayed each icon and polished vigorously, seemingly oblivious to the ongoing prayers. I wondered if she was the priest's wife. I also wondered what our congregation in Wales would do if I appeared during the bible reading and started applying Brasso to the lectern.

My meandering thoughts were halted by the sudden appearance of the verger right in front of me, glowering even more threateningly than before. In vain I adjusted my scarf and ensured my blouse was buttoned to the neck. His eyes travelled downwards; I adjusted my skirt so that it now covered most of my calves. I could see that I had not interpreted his wishes correctly. What was I doing wrong? I was soon to find out. A pair of brown gnarled hands reached down to my ankles and firmly uncrossed them. I was mortified. He was relieved at our decision to walk out and steered us to the door. I made a mental note to write to Lonely Planet and Rough Guide to Greece and warn future travellers of the apparent sin of crossing your legs in church. I knew that there were some countries where it was not done to expose the dirtiest part of your body to anyone else, let alone God. Now, in any church, both at home and abroad I sit with both feet firmly soles down on the floor, and have not suffered another eviction.

However I have been sent home from a parish party to change into more appropriate clothing. As it was a post-Christmas party in the local pub I decided to dress seasonally and put on the red satin jacket that I had worn at a recent wedding. As I entered the room an elderly lady at the raffle table took me aside, with the words, 'Go home and get changed, dear. You look like a prostitute.'

From that night on I never wore it in the parish. However, I did take it with me on a hymn-writers' weekend, and wore it to church on Palm Sunday. Michael had always liked seeing me in red; the men on the hymn course also liked it. As we assembled in the pews one of the men whispered, 'Like your jacket, Margaret.'

'Oh – my prostitute jacket!' I replied, in a voice louder than I had meant to use. The pre-service prayers of the devout had been rudely interrupted. Every one turned to stare.

'I'll explain about it at dinner time,' I murmured, sotto voce.

I had not banked on our group having to share the dining room with a group of very strait-laced Christians. We had tried to entice them into conversation, but they remained aloof and po-faced. The only excitement in their lives came when my friends turned to me and said, 'Now then Margaret, tell us how you came to be a prostitute.'

At least three of the holy brethren choked on their gravy; the others cast their eyes downwards. I expect they were praying for my redemption.

I still wear my red satin jacket from time to time, but never at a parish party, and never teamed with black fishnet tights and I make sure I keep well away from street corners.

I didn't take the jacket to Russia, even though it was the year we were celebrating our Ruby wedding. We had booked in for a group holiday, 'Winter Russia', flying to Moscow, and then taking the train to St. Petersburg. It was in early January and coincided with the Orthodox Christmas. We had made a mental note not to eat any symbolic bread buns or to cross our legs in church. In fact it would have been a physical impossibility for me to have heaved one leg over another, encased as they were in two pairs of tights, one pair of long johns, track suit bottoms, waterproof trousers, two pairs of thick socks and walking boots.

We were amazed at the number of people continuously shuffling forward in the snow in long queues to get into the churches. Outside, in Red Square, families were exchanging Christmas greetings. It was so cold that I thought their lips would stick together. My eyelashes and the hairs in my nose were like frozen pine needles, and feeling had long since left my toes and fingers. Yet the hardy Muscovites were seemingly oblivious to the temperature, and were eating – indeed enjoying – ice cream! We could manage about 15 minutes in the great outdoors before having to dodge down into their superb Metro to thaw out before our next foray into the snowy streets.

We survived, and thoroughly enjoyed Moscow and St. Petersburg, despite two accidents on the ice and a dramatic theft of passport and money from members of our group on the station platform that had turned into a skating rink. We had realised it was very cold, but not until we caught sight of a British paper did we realise just how cold.

'Russia faces coldest winter since 1940'

'Babies dying in hospitals due to breakdown in heating system in Russia's ice age. Urgent demand for hot water bottles to be brought to maternity hospitals.'

Our friends were understandably anxious at how we were surviving temperatures plummeting to minus 35 degrees Celsius. Our family knew that the blue long johns would have come into their own once again.

These long johns had featured unexpectedly in a Christmas sermon, in which Michael had wanted a visual aid to illustrate the carefully chosen gift that God gave to us at Christmas in the form of His Son. To illustrate his sermon he had picked, from under our Christmas tree, the most beautifully wrapped present. He had no idea what was inside.

The sermon was preached at the midnight service. I held my breath as Michael toyed with the idea of opening the present in the pulpit; I knew what was inside. Pauline had phoned me from Cardiff to ask if Dad would like some long johns for our forthcoming holiday to Switzerland. I breathed more easily when Michael, realising he had to use the same sermon at two other services, declined to open the parcel – leaving the congregation agog to know what was inside. At the third service I prayed that he would not open it. I knew Mrs Evans would hate to see her red poinsettias, which encircled the pulpit, draped with a pair of blue woolly long johns. My prayers were heard. Then I heard Michael saying, 'I won't open this present now – but I know it will have been carefully chosen and given in love. This afternoon it will be in pride of place on the mantelpiece.'

The telephone was busy on Boxing Day.

'I just wondered what was in your parcel, vicar?'

The tale of the blue long johns soon circulated the diocese. People will be pleased to know that they are still going strong twenty-one years later.

I fear that they will be in use again soon. I have just seen Michael reading his way avidly through a travel book. Its title? 'Trans-Siberian Railway'.

I rather think I will not be going away with the vicar on this occasion. I'll content myself with reading up about it, planning his itinerary, and waving him on his way.

What will I do while he's away? I'll stay at home and start my next book: 'Vicariously to Vladivostok.'